The Mobile App Mastery

Innovate, Design, and Thrive in the App Ecosystem

Marcus Devlin

Table of Contents

INTRODUCTION **6**

CHAPTER I. Understanding the App Ecosystem **8**

Evolution of Mobile Apps 8

Key Players in the App Ecosystem 10

Trends and Challenges 13

CHAPTER II. Ideation and Innovation **17**

Identifying Opportunities 17

Idea Generation Techniques 20

Validating App Ideas 23

Understanding User Needs and Preferences 26

CHAPTER III. Design Principles for Mobile Apps **30**

User-Centered Design Approach 30

UI/UX Best Practices 33

Design Tools and Technologies 35

Accessibility and Inclusivity in App Design 39

CHAPTER IV. Development Fundamentals **43**

Choosing the Right Development Platform 43

Programming Languages and Frameworks 46

Agile Development Methodologies 49

Testing and Debugging Strategies 52

CHAPTER V. Monetization Strategies **56**

Freemium vs. Premium Models 56

In-App Purchases and Subscriptions 59

Advertising and Sponsorships 61

Alternative Revenue Streams 64

CHAPTER VI. Marketing and Promotion 68

App Store Optimization (ASO) 68

Social Media Marketing 70

Influencer Partnerships 73

Public Relations and Press Coverage 76

CHAPTER VII. Launching Your App 80

Pre-launch Strategies 80

App Store Submission Process 83

Post-launch Monitoring and Optimization 86

CHAPTER VIII. User Engagement and Retention 89

Building a Community Around Your App 89

Push Notifications and In-App Messaging 92

Feedback Loops and Continuous Improvement 95

CHAPTER IX. Scaling Your App Business 99

Scaling Infrastructure and Resources 99

Expanding to New Markets 102

Strategic Partnerships and Acquisitions 104

Managing Growth and Sustainability 107

CHAPTER X. Case Studies 111

Successful Mobile App Stories 111

Lessons Learned from Failures 113

Analyzing Industry Trends 116

CHAPTER XI. Looking Ahead **119**

Emerging Technologies and Trends 119

Future of Mobile Apps 121

Recommendations for Aspiring App Entrepreneurs ... 124

CONCLUSION **127**

INTRODUCTION

Mobile applications are become an essential part of our everyday lives in the connected society we live in today. The possibilities seem limitless, from managing our finances to ordering food, from staying connected with loved ones to accessing entertainment. The app ecosystem has grown exponentially, presenting unprecedented opportunities and formidable challenges for entrepreneurs, developers, and businesses alike. In this dynamic landscape, mastering the art of mobile app development is paramount to success.

Welcome to "The Mobile App Mastery: Innovate, Design, and Thrive in the App Ecosystem." This book is your all-in-one resource for understanding the complex world of mobile apps, giving you the tools you need to develop successful apps and prosper in the competitive app store.

We will journey through each stage of the app development lifecycle—from ideation to launch and beyond—in the pages that follow. Whether you're a seasoned developer seeking to enhance your skills or a budding entrepreneur with a groundbreaking app idea, this book will equip you with the knowledge, tools, and strategies necessary to succeed.

We begin by exploring the evolution of mobile apps and the key players shaping the app ecosystem today. Understanding the landscape is crucial for identifying opportunities and staying ahead of trends. From there, we delve into the creative process of ideation and innovation, guiding you through techniques for generating and validating app ideas while keeping user needs at the forefront.

Design is a cornerstone of successful mobile apps, and we dedicate a section to exploring design principles, user experience best practices, and accessibility considerations. Armed with this knowledge, you'll be able to create apps that look stunning and deliver exceptional user experiences.

Development fundamentals, monetization strategies, marketing tactics, user engagement techniques, and scaling strategies are all covered in depth, providing you with a comprehensive toolkit for building and growing your app business.

Throughout the book, we'll draw insights from real-world case studies, successful app stories, and industry trends, offering practical advice and actionable strategies to apply to your projects.

Whether you're an aspiring app developer, a seasoned entrepreneur, or anyone interested in the world of mobile apps, "The Mobile App Mastery" is your roadmap to success in the vibrant and ever-evolving app ecosystem. Let's embark on this journey together and unlock the full potential of mobile app innovation.

CHAPTER I

Understanding the App Ecosystem

Evolution of Mobile Apps

The evolution of mobile apps represents one of the most important technological advancements in the digital era, fundamentally transforming how individuals interact with technology and each other. From the inception of simple applications designed for basic phones to the sophisticated, multifunctional apps used on today's smartphones, the mobile app development journey has been marked by rapid innovation and growth. This section explores the trajectory of mobile apps, highlighting key developments, technological advancements, and their impact on society.

In the early stages of mobile technology, applications were rudimentary, often built into the device and limited to functions such as a calculator, calendar, and contact book. However, the launch of the first smartphones marked a pivotal moment in the evolution of mobile apps. These devices, equipped with operating systems similar to those of computers, provided a platform for developing and using more sophisticated software. The introduction of app stores, such as Apple's App Store in 2008 and Google's Play Store, revolutionized how apps were distributed and accessed, creating a new economy and opening up vast opportunities for developers and businesses.

The significance of this new distribution channel cannot be overstated. It democratized app development, allowing independent developers and small companies to reach a global audience with their creations. This led to an explosion in the number and variety of apps available, catering to almost every conceivable need and interest. From gaming and entertainment to productivity and health, apps played a central role in people's lives, offering convenience and new ways to learn, work, and connect with others.

The development of mobile apps has been fueled by advancements in technology. Improved smartphone hardware, such as faster processors, better graphics, and increased storage, has allowed for more complex and powerful apps. Moreover, the advent of high-speed internet and the expansion of mobile broadband have enabled apps that require real-time data exchange and streaming, such as video calls and online gaming. Furthermore, integrating technologies like GPS, NFC (Near Field Communication), and various sensors has led to the development of apps that interact with the physical world in innovative ways, such as location-based services, fitness trackers, and contactless payments.

Another significant aspect of the evolution of mobile apps is the shift towards cloud computing. This has allowed apps to offer services that store as well as process data on remote servers, providing users with access to their information from any device and enhancing the functionality of apps through the power of cloud-based computing resources. This shift has also facilitated the development of machine learning and artificial intelligence (AI) features in apps, enabling personalized experiences, intelligent recommendations, and advanced voice recognition capabilities.

The impact of mobile apps on society has been profound. They have changed how people communicate, shop, access information, and entertain themselves. Social media apps have redefined social interactions, creating new opportunities for connectivity while raising concerns about privacy and spreading misinformation. E-commerce apps have transformed consumer behavior, making online shopping more accessible and convenient. Moreover, mobile apps have become crucial tools for education, healthcare, and business, providing innovative solutions to traditional challenges and increasing efficiency.

However, the rapid evolution of mobile apps has not been without its challenges. Issues related to security, privacy, and data protection have become increasingly prominent. The vast amount of personal information processed by mobile apps has raised concerns about how this data is used and shared. Additionally, the dominance of a few app stores has sparked debates about market competition and the control over app distribution and monetization.

In conclusion, the development of mobile apps has been marked by both significant societal influence and quick technological improvement. Mobile applications have become an essential part of contemporary culture, ranging from basic tools to intricate platforms that influence daily life. We can expect mobile apps to evolve further as technology advances, offering new possibilities and challenges. The future of mobile apps will likely be marked by continued technological innovation, such as augmented reality and AI, further changing how we interact with the world around us. As we look forward, it is clear that mobile apps will be pivotal in the digital landscape, influencing how we use technology and live our lives.

Key Players in the App Ecosystem

The dynamic and multifaceted app ecosystem is shaped by various key players whose contributions and interactions define the landscape of mobile technology and software development. This ecosystem is not just about the apps themselves but encompasses the networks, platforms, developers, and consumers interacting within it, creating a vibrant and constantly evolving digital environment. This section delves into the roles of these key players, examining how they contribute to the ecosystem and influence its development and sustainability.

At the heart of the app ecosystem are the platform providers, such as Apple with its iOS operating system and Google with Android. These companies are foundational to the ecosystem, providing the operating systems that power billions of mobile devices worldwide. Additionally, they oversee the Google Play Store and the Apple App Store, two major app distribution platforms that are essential for finding, downloading, and using apps. These platforms not only set the technical standards and guidelines for app development but also shape the economic model of the ecosystem through revenue sharing policies and advertising frameworks. The types of apps that can be developed and how they are marketed are directly influenced by their development tools and policies, which in turn shapes the application landscape.

Developers, ranging from individual hobbyists to large corporations, are the creative force behind the apps. They utilize the platforms and tools the operating system developers provide to bring various applications to the market. These can range from simple utilities and games to complex enterprise solutions and social networks. Developers must navigate the technical requirements, user expectations, and monetization strategies within the constraints and opportunities of the app stores. Their innovation and responsiveness to consumer demands drive the continuous evolution of the app offerings, making them a critical component of the ecosystem.

Third-party service providers also play a significant role in the app ecosystem. These include cloud computing services, analytics platforms, advertising networks, and tool developers that offer services to support app functionality, distribution, and monetization. For example, cloud services enable apps to store and process data remotely, enhancing their capabilities without requiring extensive resources on the device itself. Analytics services provide developers with insights into app performance and user behavior, helping to refine and improve offerings. Advertising networks, on the other hand, offer a vital revenue stream for many apps, facilitating targeted advertising based on user data and behavior.

Consumers, or users, are the driving force behind the demand for mobile apps. Their preferences, feedback, and usage patterns influence app development priorities and trends. Consumers decide which apps succeed or fail based on their adoption and use, making them a powerful influence on the ecosystem. User expectations for functionality, usability, privacy, and security guide developers in creating and updating apps. Moreover, the feedback and reviews provided by users in app stores play a crucial role in the discovery and success of new apps, influencing other users' decisions and developers' reputations.

Regulators and policy makers also impact the app ecosystem, though indirectly. Their decisions regarding privacy, data protection, and digital commerce can significantly affect how apps are developed, marketed, and monetized. Design and development objectives are influenced, for example, by laws like the GDPR (General Data Protection Regulation) in the European Union, which place stringent standards on how personal data is gathered, used, and safeguarded by applications. Similarly, antitrust investigations into the practices of platform providers can lead to changes in app store policies, affecting how apps are distributed and monetized.

Lastly, the tech community, including educational institutions, research organizations, and industry forums, contributes to the app ecosystem by fostering innovation and skills development. These entities provide the research, education, and collaboration opportunities that fuel technological advancements and the professional development of developers. By pushing the boundaries of what is possible and training the next generation of developers, the tech community ensures the continuous evolution and vitality of the app ecosystem.

In conclusion, the app ecosystem is a complex and dynamic network of interactions among various key players, including platform providers, developers, third-party service providers, consumers, regulators, and the broader tech community. Each group plays a particular role in shaping the ecosystem, influencing everything from the technical standards and economic models to the types of apps available and how they are used. The success of the app ecosystem depends on the balance and collaboration among these players, as they navigate the challenges and opportunities of the digital age. As technology and society evolve, so will the roles and relationships within the app ecosystem, driving innovation and adaptation in this vibrant and critical domain of the digital economy.

Trends and Challenges

The app ecosystem, a dynamic and ever-evolving landscape, is shaped by ongoing trends and faced with numerous challenges that influence its direction and sustainability. Developers, platform providers, and other stakeholders navigate a complex web of opportunities and obstacles as technology advances and user preferences shift. This section explores the current trends and challenges within the app ecosystem, highlighting their implications for the future of mobile technology and digital interaction.

The growing utilization of artificial intelligence (AI) as well as machine learning (ML) in apps is one of the biggest developments. These technologies are being used to personalize user experiences, improve app functionality, and create more intelligent and responsive systems. AI-driven personal assistants, recommendation engines, and predictive text are just a few examples of how these technologies enhance app capabilities. However, integrating AI and ML presents challenges, including data privacy concerns, the need for large datasets for training algorithms, and the technical complexity of developing and maintaining AI-driven features.

Another trend is the move towards cloud-based apps and services, allowing for more powerful and efficient app functionalities that are not limited by the device's hardware. Cloud computing enables apps to store and process data remotely, facilitating features like real-time collaboration, seamless cross-device experiences, and substantial data analysis capabilities. Despite these advantages, this trend raises issues connected to data security and privacy, as well as the reliance on constant internet connectivity, which can exclude users in areas with poor connectivity.

The proliferation of cross-platform development tools is also reshaping the app ecosystem. These tools let developers to write code once and deploy it across multiple operating systems, reducing development time and costs. This trend particularly benefits smaller developers looking to reach a wider audience. However, it also poses challenges, such as the potential for performance issues and the difficulty of optimizing apps for each platform's unique features and guidelines.

User privacy as well as data protection have become paramount concerns within the app ecosystem. With increasing awareness of data breaches and misuse, users are more cautious about the apps they download and the permissions they grant. This concern has led to stricter regulations, such as the GDPR or General Data Protection Regulation, in the European Union, imposing new requirements on app developers and platform providers. Navigating these regulations while maintaining user trust and providing valuable services is a significant challenge for stakeholders in the ecosystem.

Monetization strategies within the app ecosystem are also evolving. The traditional models, such as paid downloads, in-app purchases, and advertising, are being supplemented or replaced by subscription services, freemium models, and in-app advertising that respects user privacy. Finding the proper balance between generating revenue and providing user value without compromising the user experience is a persistent challenge for developers.

The democratization of app development, facilitated by easier access to development tools and platforms, has led to an explosion in the number of apps available. While this inclusivity fosters innovation and variety, it also saturates the market, making it harder for developers to stand out and for users to find quality apps. The app discovery process is, therefore, a significant challenge, with developers often relying on app store optimization (ASO) strategies and marketing efforts to increase visibility.

Accessibility and inclusivity remain crucial challenges within the app ecosystem. Ensuring that apps are usable by people with disabilities, such as those requiring screen readers or alternative input methods, is essential for creating an inclusive digital environment. Moreover, the need for apps to cater to diverse cultural and linguistic needs is increasingly recognized, demanding a more nuanced approach to app design and localization.

Finally, the rapid pace of technological change and the emergence of new platforms, such as wearable devices and the Internet of Things (IoT), present both opportunities and challenges. Developers must constantly update their skills and adapt their apps to function across various devices and use cases. Ensuring compatibility, maintaining security, and providing seamless user experiences across these platforms require significant effort and innovation.

In conclusion, the app ecosystem is characterized by its dynamic nature, driven by technological advancements and shifting user expectations. The trends towards AI and ML integration, cloud-based services, cross-platform development, and evolving monetization strategies reflect the ecosystem's adaptability and innovation. However, these trends also bring challenges, including privacy and data protection concerns, market saturation, accessibility issues, and the need for constant technological adaptation. Navigating these trends and challenges requires a collaborative effort among developers, platform providers, regulators, and users to ensure the ecosystem thrives and positively impacts the digital and physical worlds. As we look to the future, the ability of stakeholders to address these challenges while leveraging new opportunities will shape the trajectory of the app ecosystem and its role in our daily lives.

CHAPTER II

Ideation and Innovation

Identifying Opportunities

Identifying opportunities within the app ecosystem requires a nuanced understanding of its dynamics, including technological trends, user behavior, market gaps, and emerging needs. The app ecosystem is a vibrant and ever-evolving landscape where the rapid pace of innovation opens up new avenues for entrepreneurs, developers, and businesses to create value. This section explores various strategies for identifying opportunities in this competitive yet lucrative field, focusing on market research, technological advancements, user-centric design, and strategic partnerships.

Market research is foundational in identifying opportunities within the app ecosystem. By analyzing current trends, consumer preferences, and competitive offerings, stakeholders can uncover underserved niches or areas ripe for innovation. This involves looking at what is popular now and predicting future trends and user needs. For instance, as society becomes more health-conscious, there is a growing demand for wellness and mental health apps. Similarly, the increased remote work and learning has spurred interest in productivity and collaboration tools. Market research that combines data analysis with a forward-looking perspective can reveal opportunities for apps that address emerging lifestyles and societal shifts.

Technological advancements are another fertile ground for identifying opportunities. The app ecosystem is closely tied to the development of new technologies, such as augmented reality (or AR), virtual reality (or VR), artificial intelligence (or AI), and blockchain. Each of these technologies opens up new possibilities for app development. For example, AR and VR can transform educational apps by providing immersive learning experiences, while AI can enhance personalization and efficiency in everything from fitness to finance apps. Blockchain technology offers opportunities for secure, decentralized apps in fields such as finance, logistics, and identity verification. Staying abreast of technological trends and understanding their potential applications can enable developers and businesses to pioneer innovative solutions that meet evolving user needs.

User-centric design is crucial in identifying and capitalizing on opportunities in the app ecosystem. This approach involves profoundly understanding the user's needs, pain points, and behaviors to create real value solutions. Engaging with potential users through surveys, interviews, and usability testing can uncover insights into what users truly want and need, often revealing gaps in the market. For example, there may be a demand for more intuitive and accessible financial management tools for non-experts or social networking apps prioritizing privacy and meaningful interactions. By putting the user at the center of the development process, developers can create apps that not only meet existing needs but also anticipate and shape future demand.

Strategic partnerships also present a significant opportunity within the app ecosystem. Collaborating with other businesses, technology providers, or content creators can open up new app development and distribution possibilities. For example, an app developer might partner with a hardware manufacturer to create apps optimized for a new device or with a content provider to offer exclusive content within an app. Partnerships can also extend an app's reach and functionality, such as integrating payment solutions or transportation services. By combining resources and expertise, partners can create more comprehensive and compelling offerings that meet users' needs innovatively.

Another area ripe for exploration is the integration of apps into the Internet of Things (IoT). As more devices become connected, there is a growing opportunity for apps that manage, analyze, and enhance the IoT experience. Apps that can seamlessly integrate various smart devices in the home, workplace, or city infrastructure can offer users more control, efficiency, and insights into their environment. Developing for the IoT requires a deep understanding of networking, data security, and user interface design, but the potential to transform everyday life makes it a promising area for innovation.

Furthermore, sustainability and social impact are increasingly important to consumers, presenting opportunities for apps that contribute to environmental protection, social justice, and community engagement. Apps that promote sustainable living practices, provide platforms for activism, or facilitate charitable giving are meeting a growing demand for technology that serves individual needs and contributes to the greater good. Developers who can align their offerings with these values have the opportunity to tap into a passionate and engaged user base.

Finally, the app ecosystem's global nature offers localization and cultural customization opportunities. Apps thoughtfully adapted to different languages, cultures, and regional needs can capture significant markets that global players often overlook. Understanding local customs, regulations, and consumer behaviors can guide the development of apps that resonate with users in specific geographic markets. This approach broadens an app's potential audience and contributes to a more diverse and inclusive digital landscape.

In conclusion, the app ecosystem is rich with opportunities for those who are prepared to explore emerging trends, leverage new technologies, design with the user in mind, and form strategic partnerships. Success in this competitive environment requires a proactive and innovative approach, focusing on creating value for users and addressing unmet needs. By staying attuned to the shifts in technology, society, and consumer behavior, developers, entrepreneurs, and businesses can identify and capitalize on the vast opportunities within the app ecosystem. As technology evolves and integrate more deeply into our lives, the potential for impactful and transformative apps is boundless, offering endless possibilities for those ready to seize them.

Idea Generation Techniques

Idea generation in the app ecosystem is critical for developers, entrepreneurs, and businesses aiming to innovate and capture value in a highly competitive market. Generating viable, innovative app ideas requires an understanding of current market trends and technologies and a creative approach to problem-solving and opportunity identification. This section explores various techniques for idea generation within the app ecosystem, emphasizing the importance of user-centric design, market analysis, technological exploration, and creative thinking.

One foundational technique for generating app ideas is to start with user needs and pain points. This user-centric approach involves deep research into the target audience's daily challenges, desires, and behaviors. Developers can engage with potential users through surveys, interviews, and observation to uncover unmet needs or frustrations with current solutions. This direct insight into the user's world can reveal opportunities for new apps or improvements to existing ones that better serve user needs. For example, recognizing a common pain point in managing personal finances might lead to developing a more intuitive and helpful budgeting app.

Market analysis is another crucial technique for idea generation. By examining the current app landscape, including competitors, market trends, and emerging sectors, developers can identify gaps in the market or areas ripe for innovation. This involves looking at the most popular apps and analyzing user reviews, industry reports, and technology trends. Understanding what is currently available and where users express dissatisfaction can highlight opportunities for differentiation and innovation. For instance, noticing a lack of effective tools for remote team collaboration in creative industries could inspire the development of an app tailored to this niche.

Exploring emerging technologies is a technique that can lead to groundbreaking app ideas. Staying abreast of advancements in artificial intelligence, augmented reality, blockchain, and other cutting-edge technologies can inspire new app functionalities and experiences. Developers might experiment with these technologies to understand their capabilities and limitations, leading to innovative applications that leverage tech in novel ways. For example, augmented reality technology can offer unique opportunities in educational apps, providing immersive learning experiences that were previously impossible.

Brainstorming and ideation sessions are classic techniques that foster team creativity and idea generation. These sessions encourage the free flow of ideas, allowing participants to develop on each other's thoughts and explore diverse perspectives. Employing structured brainstorming methods, such as SCAMPER or

(Substitute, Combine, Adapt, Modify, Put to another use, Eliminate, Reverse) or mind mapping, can help organize thoughts and uncover connections between seemingly disparate ideas. These collaborative sessions can spark innovative concepts by encouraging out-of-the-box thinking and exploring how a new app could combine or adapt different features or services.

Applying design thinking to app idea generation is a method that emphasizes empathy with users, creative problem-solving, and iterative testing. This approach involves deeply understanding the user's experience, defining the problem clearly, ideating solutions, prototyping, and testing. Through this process, assumptions are challenged, and insights are gained that can lead to innovative app solutions tailored to real user needs. Design thinking encourages a user-focused approach, ensuring that the app idea is not only technologically feasible but also desirable and viable from a user perspective.

Leveraging data analytics and user feedback from existing apps can also be a powerful technique for generating new app ideas. Analyzing user behavior, preferences, and feedback data can uncover trends and pain points that may not be immediately obvious. This analysis can inspire ideas for new features, services, or entirely new apps that address these insights. For instance, if data from a fitness app reveals that users are mainly engaged with social challenges, this could indicate an opportunity to develop a new app focused on community-driven fitness challenges.

Looking outside the app ecosystem to other industries and disciplines can also stimulate innovative app ideas. Inspiration can come from analyzing how challenges are addressed in different fields, such as healthcare, education, or entertainment, and considering how similar approaches could be adapted for the digital space. This cross-pollination of ideas can result in distinct app concepts that bring novel solutions to the market.

Finally, setting up a conducive environment for creativity and innovation is essential for effective idea generation. This means developing a culture that encourages experimentation, tolerates failure, and supports continuous learning. Providing time and resources for team members to explore new technologies, attend workshops, and work on passion projects can foster an innovative mindset and lead to discovering new app ideas.

In conclusion, generating app ideas in the ever-evolving app ecosystem requires a multifaceted approach that combines user-centric research, market analysis, exploration of new technologies, and creative thinking. By employing various techniques, from direct user engagement and market analysis to brainstorming sessions and cross-industry inspiration, developers and businesses can uncover unique opportunities for innovation. Embracing a culture that values creativity, experimentation, and user empathy can further enhance the idea-generation process, leading to the development of apps that meet not only current market needs but also anticipate future trends and user desires. The secret to success in the competitive app market lies in continuously exploring, learning, and adapting, ensuring that new app ideas are both innovative and aligned with the evolving digital landscape.

Validating App Ideas

Validating app ideas is a crucial step in the development process, ensuring that the time and resources invested in building an app are directed towards a solution that meets real user needs and has a viable market. This process involves a series of strategic evaluations to assess the app concept's feasibility, desirability, and viability before full- scale development begins. This section explores various approaches to validating app ideas, emphasizing the importance of user feedback, market analysis, prototyping, and financial modeling in making informed decisions about app development.

The first step in validating an app idea is to conduct thorough market research. This involves analyzing the competitive landscape, identifying direct and indirect competitors, and understanding the target audience's characteristics and behaviors. Market research helps to confirm whether there is a demand for the app, the saturation level of the market, and potential gaps that the app could fill. By examining trends, user reviews of similar apps, and market data, developers can gauge the app's potential for success and refine their value proposition to meet user needs better.

Engaging with potential users early and often is another critical component of the validation process. This can be gained through surveys, interviews, and focus groups to acquire insights directly from the target audience. The objective is to understand their pain points, preferences, and the usability of the proposed solution. User feedback is invaluable in assessing whether the app idea solves a real problem or fulfills a desire in a way that resonates with potential users. It can also reveal the most essential features to the target audience, guiding the prioritization of development efforts.

Establishing a minimum viable product, also known as MVP, is a powerful approach to validating app ideas. An MVP is the simplest version of the app that still provides its core functionality and value. By launching an MVP, developers can test their hypotheses about the market and user needs in a real-world setting, gathering data on how actual users interact with the app. This approach allows for iterative development, where the app is continuously refined based on user feedback and usage patterns. The MVP process helps to minimize risks and investment by focusing on building and enhancing features that users truly value.

Prototyping is another effective method for validation, especially in the early stages of app development. Prototypes can range from simple wireframes to interactive models that simulate the app's functionality. Prototyping enables developers and stakeholders to visualize the app's design and user experience, facilitating early feedback and identifying potential issues. It's a cost-effective way to explore different design concepts and user flows without needing full-scale development. Developers can validate the app's usability and appeal by testing prototypes with potential users before committing to more extensive development efforts.

Financial modeling is essential for validating the economic viability of an app idea. This involves creating revenue, costs, and profitability projections based on various assumptions about the app's market penetration, pricing strategy, and operating expenses. Financial models help to assess whether the app can generate a sustainable revenue stream and achieve a return on investment. They are critical for making informed resource allocation decisions and attracting potential investors or partners.

Leveraging analytics and data from existing products or services can also aid in validating app ideas. If the app is an extension or enhancement of an existing product, analyzing user behavior and feedback can provide insights into the potential demand and design considerations for the app. Data analytics can uncover patterns and preferences that inform the app's development, ensuring it aligns with user expectations and market needs.

Social validation, through platforms like social media or crowdfunding sites, can be useful for gauging interest in the app idea. Developers can measure the level of enthusiasm and potential market size by presenting the concept to a broad audience and soliciting feedback or financial support. Crowdfunding campaigns, in particular, can serve as a litmus test for the app's appeal and provide initial funding to support development.

Finally, conducting a pre-launch marketing campaign can help validate interest and build anticipation for the app. This can include creating a landing page, collecting email sign-ups, and engaging with potential users through social media and content marketing. The response to these efforts can provide valuable insights into the market's readiness and interest in the app, guiding further development and marketing strategies.

In conclusion, validating app ideas is a multi-faceted process that involves market research, user engagement, prototyping, financial analysis, and strategic testing. By thoroughly assessing the app concept's feasibility, desirability, and viability, developers can mitigate risks and focus their efforts on creating solutions that genuinely meet user needs and have a strong market potential. Validation is not a one-time task but an ongoing process that continues through the development lifecycle, ensuring that the app remains relevant and valuable to its intended audience. Through diligent validation, developers can increase their chances of launching successful apps that resonate with users and stand out in the competitive app ecosystem.

Understanding User Needs and Preferences

Understanding user needs and preferences is a cornerstone of successful app development. In a digital landscape crowded with millions of apps, the ones that stand out are those designed with a deep understanding of their target users. This section delves into the significance of comprehending user needs and preferences, outlining strategies for gathering and implementing user insights to develop apps that resonate with and provide real value to their intended audience.

At its core, understanding user needs and preferences involves identifying the problems users face, their desires, how they interact with technology, and what they value in an app. This understanding ensures that the app not only addresses a real demand but does so in a way that enhances the user's experience, engagement, and satisfaction. Uncovering these insights is multifaceted, involving research, analysis, and continuous feedback loops.

Research is the first step in understanding user needs. This can take many forms, from quantitative surveys and analytics to qualitative interviews and focus groups. Surveys can provide a broad overview of user demographics, preferences, and behavior patterns. Analytics from existing apps or web platforms can reveal how users interact with digital products, highlighting popular features and potential pain points. Qualitative methods, including interviews and focus groups, offer deep insights into the user's experiences, motivations, and attitudes, providing a rich context for interpreting quantitative data. Together, these research methods paint a comprehensive picture of the user's world, guiding the development of app features and interfaces that meet their needs.

Personas and user stories are valuable tools for synthesizing research findings into actionable insights. Personas are fictional characters representing the app's target users, created based on research data. They help developers and designers empathize with users, keeping their needs and preferences at the forefront of the development process. User stories translate these needs into specific features and functionalities, describing what users want to achieve through the app. By grounding development in personas and user stories, teams can ensure that the app remains user-centric at every stage.

User experience (or UX) and user interface (or UI) design are critical to addressing user needs and preferences. UX design focuses on the app's overall experience, including how easily and effectively users can complete tasks. UI design, on the other hand, concerns the app's visual and interactive elements. Both disciplines rely on understanding user preferences to create intuitive, engaging, and accessible designs. This includes considerations like ease of navigation, aesthetic appeal, and adaptability to various devices and screen sizes. Effective UX/UI design enhances user satisfaction and can significantly impact the app's adoption and retention rates.

Prototyping and usability testing are essential for validating and refining the understanding of user needs. Prototypes, ranging from low-fidelity sketches to high-fidelity interactive models, allow developers to test design concepts and gather feedback before committing to full-scale development. Usability testing, in which real users interact with the prototype, provides direct insights into how users experience the app, revealing areas for improvement. This iterative design, testing, and refinement process ensures that the app evolves in response to user feedback, aligning closely with their needs and preferences.

Analytics and feedback mechanisms within the app itself offer ongoing insights into user behavior and satisfaction. By monitoring the way users interact with the app, developers can identify which features are most and least used, how users navigate through the app, and where they encounter difficulties. Feedback forms, ratings, and reviews provide direct user feedback on the app's strengths and areas for improvement. This continuous loop of data collection and analysis allows developers to update and adapt the app over time, ensuring it remains relevant and valuable to its users.

In addition to these strategies, staying attuned to broader trends in technology and society can help anticipate user needs and preferences changes. Advances in technology, shifts in social attitudes, and emerging challenges all influence what users expect and require from apps. By monitoring these trends, developers can proactively innovate, integrating new technologies and addressing evolving user demands.

In conclusion, understanding user needs and preferences is fundamental to successful app development. It requires a multi-disciplinary approach that combines research, design, testing, and ongoing analysis. By placing users at the center of the development process, developers can create apps that not only meet a specific need but do so in a way that is intuitive, engaging, and satisfying for the user. This user-centric approach enhances the chances of the app's success and contributes to a more usable, enjoyable, and meaningful digital landscape. As technology and user expectations evolve, understanding and responding to user needs will remain a key differentiator in the competitive app ecosystem.

CHAPTER III

Design Principles for Mobile Apps

User-Centered Design Approach

User-centered design (UCD) is a framework in the development of mobile apps that places the user at the forefront of the design process. This approach emphasizes understanding end users' needs, preferences, and limitations at every stage of the design and development process, making sure that the final product is functional, user-friendly, and aligned with the user's expectations. By adopting a UCD approach, developers and designers aim to create mobile apps that offer users a seamless, intuitive, and satisfying experience. This section explores the principles, processes, and benefits of adopting a user-centered design approach in mobile app development.

At the heart of user-centered design is the principle that successful apps must meet the real needs of their users. This involves thorough research to understand who the users are, what tasks they need to perform, and what challenges they face. This user research is typically conducted through various methods, including interviews, surveys, and observations, which help gather detailed insights into the user's behaviors, preferences, and environments. By grounding the design process in actual user data, developers can avoid assumptions and biases that may lead to irrelevant or difficult to use features. Once

user needs are understood, the next principle of UCD is to design with these needs in mind. This involves generating design concepts that address the identified user requirements and testing these concepts with users to gather feedback. Prototyping is a key tool in this phase, enabling designers to create tangible representations of their ideas through paper sketches or interactive digital mockups. These prototypes are then used in usability testing sessions, where real users interact with the design and provide feedback on its ease of use, effectiveness, and overall experience. This iterative design, test, and refine process ensures that the app evolves in direct response to user feedback, leading to a more user- friendly product.

Another core aspect of user-centered design is accessibility. A UCD approach requires that apps be designed to be accessible to users with an array of abilities, including those with disabilities. This means considering aspects such as color contrast, text size, voice commands, and alternative navigation methods to ensure that everyone can utilize the app. By prioritizing accessibility, designers create apps that are not only more inclusive but also more versatile and adaptable to different user contexts and preferences.

The benefits of a user-centered design approach in mobile app development are numerous. First and foremost, it leads to higher user satisfaction. When users find an app simple to use, effective in meeting their needs, and enjoyable to interact with, they are more likely to use it frequently, recommend it to others, and provide positive reviews. This user satisfaction translates into better engagement metrics, higher retention rates, and eventually, greater success for the app in the marketplace.

Furthermore, a UCD approach can significantly reduce development costs and time. By identifying and addressing user needs early in the process, developers can avoid costly revisions and rework later on. Usability testing with prototypes can uncover issues before they become embedded in the code, making them much cheaper and quicker to fix. This proactive approach to addressing user needs can streamline the development process, ensuring that efforts focus on features that users value and use.

Moreover, adopting a user-centered design approach can enhance the app's brand image and competitive advantage. In a crowded app market, apps that are known for their excellent user experience stand out and can command a loyal user base. Developers can build a strong brand reputation that attracts users and differentiates their app from competitors by demonstrating a commitment to understanding and meeting user needs.

Implementing a user-centered design approach requires a collaborative and flexible development team that values user feedback and is willing to iterate on their designs. It also requires effective communication with users, ensuring their voices are heard and understood throughout development. This may involve setting up dedicated channels for user feedback, conducting regular usability testing sessions, and actively engaging with users through social media and other platforms.

In conclusion, a user-centered design approach is essential for developing mobile apps that are functional and deeply aligned with user needs and preferences. By prioritizing the user at every stage of the design process, developers can create apps that offer a superior user experience, leading to higher satisfaction, engagement, and success in the competitive app marketplace. Adopting a UCD approach requires a commitment to thorough research, iterative design, and continuous feedback, but the benefits in regards to user satisfaction and development efficiency make it a valuable investment for any mobile app project. As the digital landscape transforms, the principles of user-centered design will remain a guiding force in creating truly designed appsgned for the people who use them.

UI/UX Best Practices

In the rapidly evolving mobile app landscape, the importance of user interface (UI) and user experience (UX) design cannot be overstated. These elements are crucial in determining an app's success or failure, as they directly affect how users perceive and interact with the app. Best UI/UX design practices are essential guidelines that help create intuitive, engaging, and effective mobile applications. This section delves into the core principles and strategies that constitute UI/UX best practices for mobile apps, focusing on simplicity, consistency, usability, accessibility, and engagement.

Simplicity is the cornerstone of effective UI/UX design. In the context of mobile apps, simplicity refers to a clean, uncluttered interface that prioritizes essential features and content. This minimalist approach make sure that users are not overwhelmed by excessive information or unnecessary functionalities, making achieving their goals easier. Design simplicity helps reduce cognitive load, which is particularly important in mobile contexts where screen space is limited. Effective use of whitespace, clear typography, and a focused content hierarchy contribute to a straightforward and pleasant user experience, encouraging longer engagement and reducing the likelihood of frustration or confusion.

Consistency is another critical aspect of UI/UX design best practices. It involves maintaining uniformity in visual elements, navigation patterns, and interaction behaviors across the app. Consistency helps in building user intuition about how the app works, making it easier for them to learn and navigate. This includes consistent use of colors, fonts, button styles, and iconography, as well as consistent placement of navigation elements. A consistent design language enhances the app's aesthetic appeal and reinforces brand identity, making the app more recognizable and trustworthy to users.

Usability encompasses the functionality and intuitiveness of an app. It's about designing an app so that users can easily use it to perform tasks efficiently and accurately. Best practices in usability involve designing clear and logical navigation systems, ensuring that interactive elements are easily recognizable and reachable, and minimizing the number of steps required to complete a task. Feedback is a crucial component of usability, where the app provides immediate and clear responses to user actions, such as visual cues when a button is pressed or an error message if something goes wrong. This direct communication helps in guiding the user through the app, making the experience more satisfying and effective.

Accessibility is a principle that ensures mobile apps are usable by people of all abilities, including those with disabilities. Best practices in accessibility include providing text alternatives for non-text content, ensuring sufficient contrast between text and background for readability, and supporting screen readers and other assistive technologies. Designing with accessibility in mind expands the app's user base and demonstrates a commitment to inclusivity and social responsibility. Furthermore, many accessibility practices, such as clear labeling and logical navigation, improve the app's overall usability for all users.

Engagement is a key objective in UI/UX design, where the aim is to captivate and retain users. Best practices to enhance engagement include personalization, where the app tailors content or functionalities to individual user preferences or behaviors, creating a more relevant and compelling experience. Another strategy is using gamification elements, such as points, badges, or challenges, to encourage interaction and loyalty.

Additionally, ensuring fast load times and smooth performance is crucial for maintaining user engagement, as users are likely to abandon apps that are slow or prone to crashing.

Testing and iteration are fundamental processes in achieving effective UI/UX design. Regular usability testing with real users provides invaluable insights into how people interact with the app, highlighting areas for improvement. This iterative design, test, and refine process ensures that the app continuously evolves to meet user needs more effectively. Tools like A/B testing can also be employed to compare different design variations, helping in making data-driven decisions about which elements enhance the user experience.

In conclusion, UI/UX best practices for mobile apps revolve around creating user-centered designs prioritizing simplicity, consistency, usability, accessibility, and engagement. By adhering to these principles, developers and designers can develop mobile applications that not only meet the functional needs of users but also provide delightful experiences that encourage long-term engagement. The key to successful UI/UX design lies in understanding the user, leveraging design best practices, and continually testing and refining the app based on user feedback and behavior. In a competitive mobile app market, excellence in UI/UX design is not just a best practice; it is a necessity for any app aiming for success and user satisfaction.

Design Tools and Technologies

In the quickly evolving world of mobile app development, the significance of design tools and technologies cannot be overstated. These tools and technologies facilitate the creation of intuitive, engaging, and aesthetically pleasing mobile applications, which are crucial for capturing and retaining users' attention in a highly competitive market.

This section explores the various design tools and technologies utilized in mobile app development, highlighting their features, benefits, and the way they contribute to the app design process.

Design tools for mobile apps range from graphic design software to prototyping tools and integrated development environments (IDEs). Adobe Photoshop and Adobe Illustrator are foundational graphic design tools used for creating and editing visual elements such as icons, graphics, and UI components. Their extensive feature sets and versatility make them indispensable for designers looking to craft detailed and high-fidelity app visuals. However, the complexity and richness of these tools require a steep learning curve, underscoring the need for designers to possess a deep understanding of graphic design principles and software functionalities.

Sketch and Adobe XD are popular among UI/UX designers for their simplicity, efficiency, and focus on user interface design. Sketch, available exclusively for Mac, offers a vector-based workflow that makes it ideal for designing high-quality interfaces and icons. Its vast library of plugins and integration with other tools streamline the design process, enhancing productivity. On the other hand, Adobe XD provides a cross-platform solution for UI/UX design, offering features for designing, prototyping, and sharing interactive user experiences. Both tools support collaborative workflows, enabling teams to work together in real-time, share feedback, and iterate designs quickly.

Figma has emerged as a powerful web-based design tool that facilitates collaborative app design. Its cloud-based nature allows designers and stakeholders to collaborate on projects from anywhere, making it highly suitable for remote teams. Figma supports the entire design process, from initial wireframing to final high-fidelity prototyping, and its intuitive interface makes it accessible to designers of every skill levels. The ability to create dynamic prototypes and share them with developers and testers streamlines the handoff process, ensuring a more seamless transition from design to development.

InVision is another collaborative design platform that enables designers to create interactive prototypes. It offers tools for user testing, feedback collection, and design communication, making it an invaluable resource for validating design concepts and ensuring usability. InVision's integration with other design and project management tools further enhances its utility, allowing for a more integrated and efficient design workflow.

Regarding mobile app design technologies, several key frameworks and libraries play a crucial role. For instance, Material Design by Google provides a comprehensive design language that offers guidelines, components, and tools for creating visually appealing and functionally robust Android apps. Its principles of material metaphors, bold graphic design, and meaningful animations guide designers in creating intuitive and engaging user experiences. Similarly, Apple's Human Interface Guidelines offer a set of design principles and resources for iOS app development, ensuring that apps not only look and feel great but also adhere to the conventions and standards expected by iOS users.

React Native and Flutter are two technologies that have significantly impacted mobile app design and development. React Native, developed by Facebook, allows for the development of native apps using JavaScript and React, enabling designers and developers to work more closely together. It offers a hot reload feature that speeds up the iteration cycle by allowing immediate viewing of changes in the app. Flutter, developed by Google, is a UI toolkit for building natively compiled mobile, web, and desktop applications from a single codebase. Its rich set of customizable widgets and fast rendering engine enable the creation of beautiful, high-performance apps with expressive and flexible UIs.

In addition to these design tools and technologies, accessibility tools such as AXE and WAVE provide essential functionalities for ensuring that mobile apps are accessible to users with disabilities. These tools analyze apps for accessibility issues, offering recommendations for improvements that comply with standards such as the Web Content Accessibility Guidelines (WCAG). Ensuring accessibility is a matter of legal compliance for many apps and a best practice that expands the app's user base and demonstrates a commitment to inclusivity.

Lastly, version control systems like Git and collaboration platforms such as GitHub or Bitbucket are crucial for managing design assets and collaborating on app projects. These technologies enable teams to track changes, revert to previous versions, and work on different aspects of the project simultaneously without overwriting each other's work. Integrating these systems with design and development workflows enhances efficiency as well as minimizes the risk of errors, ensuring a smoother app development process.

In conclusion, design tools and technologies are pivotal in developing mobile apps, offering the capabilities needed to create user-centered, aesthetically pleasing, and technically sound applications. These resources support designers and developers throughout the app creation process, from graphic design software and prototyping tools to collaborative platforms and development frameworks. By leveraging these tools and technologies, teams can enhance productivity, foster innovation, and ultimately develop mobile apps that meet and exceed user expectations. As the mobile app landscape evolves, staying abreast of the latest tools and technologies will remain essential for delivering cutting-edge app experiences.

Accessibility and Inclusivity in App Design

Accessibility and inclusivity in app design are critical considerations that are significant in developing mobile applications. These principles ensure that apps are usable and enjoyable for people of all abilities, including those with disabilities such as vision, hearing, motor, and cognitive impairments. Designing for accessibility and inclusivity expands the app's user base and demonstrates a commitment to social responsibility and equality. This section delves into the importance, strategies, and benefits of incorporating accessibility and inclusivity in app design for mobile apps.

The importance of accessibility and inclusivity in app design cannot be overstated. In today's digital age, mobile apps are essential tools for communication, education, entertainment, and daily living. Ensuring these apps are accessible to everyone, including users with disabilities, is fundamental to promoting digital inclusion. Without proper consideration for accessibility, a significant portion of the population might be excluded from using these digital resources, widening the digital divide and reinforcing social inequalities. Therefore, integrating accessibility and inclusivity principles from the outset of the app design process is crucial for creating equitable digital experiences.

There are several strategies for incorporating accessibility and inclusivity into mobile app design. First and foremost, understanding the diverse needs of users is essential. This involves recognizing how people interact with technology, considering various disabilities and how they might affect app usage. For instance, users with visual impairments may rely on screen readers to navigate an app, while those with motor impairments might need larger touch targets for easier interaction.

Following established guidelines and standards is a key strategy in designing accessible apps. The Web Content Accessibility Guidelines, also referred to as WCAG provide a comprehensive framework for making digital content accessible to people with disabilities. Although initially developed for web content, many principles and guidelines apply to mobile app design. These guidelines cover a range of recommendations, like providing text alternatives for non-text content, guaranteeing sufficient contrast ratios for text and images, and making all functionality available from a keyboard for users who cannot use a touchscreen.

Leveraging the accessibility features and tools provided by mobile operating systems is another effective strategy. IOS and Android offer built-in accessibility features, such as voice control, screen readers (VoiceOver on iOS and TalkBack on Android), magnification gestures, and more. Designing apps that are compatible with these features allows developers to tap into existing solutions that users may already be familiar with, enhancing the usability of their apps for individuals with disabilities.

Inclusive design goes beyond just addressing specific disabilities and focuses on creating usable and meaningful experiences for people with a wide range of abilities, backgrounds, and preferences. This entails adopting a flexible and adaptable approach to app design, where various user settings and preferences can be accommodated. For example, allowing users to customize text size, color schemes, and navigation layouts can make an app more accessible to individuals with low vision or cognitive impairments, as well as those who simply prefer a more personalized experience.

User testing with diverse groups is crucial for identifying and addressing accessibility and inclusivity issues in app design. Engaging with users who have disabilities in the testing process can provide invaluable insights into the real-world challenges they face when interacting with mobile apps. This direct feedback enables developers to make informed adjustments and improvements, ensuring that the app meets the needs of all users.

The benefits of prioritizing accessibility and inclusivity in app design are manifold. Firstly, it significantly expands the app's potential user base, making it accessible to a broader audience, including the millions of people worldwide who live with disabilities. This has positive social implications and can lead to increased downloads, engagement, and customer loyalty. Moreover, accessible and inclusive apps tend to have better overall usability, as the design considerations that make an app more accessible often improve the user experience for everyone. This can lead to higher satisfaction rates as well as positive reviews, enhancing the app's reputation and competitive edge.

Moreover, following accessibility guidelines is not only recommended but also mandated by law in many places. By ensuring that apps are designed with accessibility in mind, developers can avoid potential legal issues and comply with legislation such as the Americans with Disabilities Act (or ADA) in the United States or the Equality Act in the United Kingdom.

In conclusion, integrating accessibility and inclusivity into mobile app design is essential for creating digital products that are equitable, usable, and enjoyable for all users. By understanding diverse user needs, following established guidelines, leveraging built-in accessibility features, adopting inclusive design practices, and conducting thorough user testing, developers can ensure their apps cater to the broadest possible audience. The benefits of this approach extend beyond social responsibility, offering the potential for increased user engagement, market reach, and compliance with legal standards. As technology plays a central role in our lives, the importance of designing accessible and inclusive mobile apps will only grow, underscoring the need for developers to embrace these principles in their design processes.

CHAPTER IV

Development Fundamentals

Choosing the Right Development Platform

Choosing the correct mobile app development platform is a crucial decision that significantly influences a mobile application's functionality, reach, and success. This choice impacts not only the initial development process but also the long-term maintenance and scalability of the app. With various platforms available, each offering unique features, capabilities, and ecosystems, selecting the most suitable one requires a thorough understanding of the project's goals, target audience, and technical requirements. This section explores the key considerations and factors that developers and businesses should consider when choosing the right mobile app development platform.

The target audience is the first consideration in selecting a mobile app development platform. Understanding the intended users' demographics, preferences, and device usage patterns is crucial. For instance, focusing on Android app development may be the best approach if the target audience primarily uses Android devices. Conversely, if the audience is more inclined towards iOS devices, particularly in markets like the U.S. and Western Europe, then iOS development should be prioritized. In some cases, where the target audience is diverse and uses a mix of both Android and iOS devices, a cross-platform development approach may be necessary to ensure broad reach and engagement.

Another critical factor is the app's purpose and functionality. Different development platforms offer varying degrees of support for specific features and capabilities. For example, if an app requires extensive use of a device's hardware, such as sensors, cameras, or GPS, native development platforms like Android Studio for Android apps and Xcode for iOS apps might provide the most robust support. On the other hand, for apps that prioritize content delivery and require less interaction with device hardware, cross-platform frameworks like React Native, Flutter, or Xamarin might be more suitable, enabling developers to write code once and deploy it over numerous platforms.

Cost considerations also play a significant role in platform selection. Native development, while offering high performance and access to the latest platform features, can be more costly and time-consuming, as it requires developing separate apps for each operating system. Cross-platform solutions can reduce development and maintenance costs by allowing for a single codebase to be used across multiple platforms. However, it's necessary to consider the potential trade-offs in terms of performance as well as access to native APIs. Additionally, the choice of platform can affect other costs, such as app store fees, development tools, and infrastructure expenses.

The development team's expertise and experience are crucial in choosing a platform. Leveraging the existing skills of a development team can reduce the learning curve and accelerate the development process. If the team has strong skills in JavaScript, for example, a JavaScript-based cross-platform framework like React Native might be a natural fit. Conversely, if the team's strengths lie in Swift or Kotlin, focusing on native iOS or Android development could be more advantageous. The availability of developer resources, community support, and documentation for the chosen platform can also influence this decision, as they can significantly impact development efficiency and problem-solving capabilities.

Scalability and future maintenance are additional considerations. The chosen platform should be able to support the app's growth in terms of user base, functionality, and data handling. This includes evaluating the platform's support for updates, compatibility with future operating system versions, and integration with backend systems. The ease of deploying updates, fixing bugs, and adding new features are essential factors that can affect the app's long-term viability and success.

Security features offered by the development platform are paramount, especially for apps that handle sensitive user data or transactions. Platforms and frameworks with robust security features, regular updates, and a good track record of addressing vulnerabilities should be prioritized to protect user data and ensure compliance with regulatory standards like GDPR or HIPAA.

Lastly, the app's deployment and distribution strategy should influence the platform choice. Each platform has its own app store, submission guidelines, and review processes. It is essential to understand these requirements and how they align with the app's goals. For instance, iOS apps are distributed through the Apple App Store, known for its stringent review process, while Android apps are typically distributed via the Google Play Store, which has its own set of guidelines and policies. Cross-platform apps may need to navigate the requirements of multiple stores, adding complexity to the deployment process.

In conclusion, selecting the best platform for developing mobile apps is a complex choice that has to take into account a number of variables, including as the intended user base, the functionality of the app, the cost of development, the experience of the team, scalability, security, and distribution options. Developers and companies can choose a platform that not only fulfills the short-term requirements of their project but also fosters its long-term growth and success by carefully weighing these factors. Whether opting for native development to leverage platform-specific features and performance or choosing a cross-platform approach for broader reach and cost efficiency, the key is to align the choice of platform with the app's objectives and the users' needs. This strategic approach ensures the development of mobile applications that are technically sound, resonate with users, and make a distinctive impression in the competitive app store.

Programming Languages and Frameworks

The creation of mobile applications has grown more intricate and dynamic, requiring a thorough grasp of the several frameworks and programming languages that support this field of technology. These tools not only define the capabilities and performance of mobile apps but also influence development efficiency, scalability, and the ability to meet user demands. This section explores the most prominent programming languages and frameworks in mobile app development, discussing their features, benefits, as well as use cases to provide a comprehensive landscape overview.

At the forefront of mobile app development are two primary platforms: Android and iOS, each supported by distinct programming languages. Java has been the conventional language of choice for Android, known for its robustness, portability, and extensive open-source libraries and community support. Java enables developers to create high-performance Android apps with complex functionalities. However, Kotlin, a newer language introduced by Google as the official language for Android development, has gained popularity for its concise syntax, safety features, and interoperability with Java. Kotlin minimizes the amount of boilerplate code, making it a more efficient option for modern Android applications.

iOS app development, on the other hand, has been dominated by Objective-C, a language that provided the foundation for iOS apps with its dynamic runtime and object-oriented capabilities. Despite its power, Objective-C's complexity and aging syntax led to the introduction of Swift by Apple. Swift has rapidly become the preferred language for iOS development due to its ease of use, safety features, and performance. Swift's modern syntax simplifies code writing and maintenance, making it accessible to beginners as well as experienced developers.

Beyond platform-specific languages, there has been a significant shift towards cross-platform development frameworks allowing a single codebase to produce apps for both Android and iOS. React Native, developed by Facebook, utilizes JavaScript, one of web development's most widely used languages, to create native apps. React Native's component-based architecture and hot reloading feature enhance developer productivity, while its vast ecosystem of libraries and tools supports the creation of complex applications.

Another notable cross-platform framework is Flutter, introduced by Google. Flutter uses the Dart programming language, which is optimized for UI construction and offers a reactive framework. Flutter's unique approach to rendering allows developers to create highly customized and visually appealing interfaces. Its single codebase can be compiled directly to native code, ensuring high performance across both platforms.

Xamarin, a framework that leverages .NET and C#, is another option for cross-platform development. Xamarin apps are built using C#, a language known for its simplicity and power, allowing developers to share code across platforms while maintaining native performance and visual consistency. Xamarin's integration with Visual Studio, a popular development environment, streamlines the development process, making it a compelling choice for developers familiar with the Microsoft ecosystem.

The choice of programming language and framework significantly impacts mobile app development. Java and Kotlin are essential for developers focused on Android, offering a range of tools and libraries tailored to the platform. With its modern features and Apple support, Swift is indispensable for creating intuitive and efficient iOS applications. For projects aiming to reach a broader audience across both platforms, React Native and Flutter provide potent solutions for cross-platform development, allowing for faster deployment and reduced costs.

In addition to these languages and frameworks, the importance of backend technologies cannot be overlooked. Node.js, for instance, is widely used for server-side operations in mobile apps, offering a non-blocking I/O model that ensures scalability and efficiency. Similarly, Firebase, a platform developed by Google, provides a comprehensive suite of backend services including real-time databases, authentication, and analytics, facilitating rapid development and deployment of mobile apps.

As mobile technology evolves, so do the languages and frameworks supporting app development. The emergence of machine learning, augmented reality, and the Internet of Things (or IoT) introduces new challenges as well as opportunities, requiring developers to adapt and learn continuously. For instance, integrating machine learning models in mobile apps, enabled by frameworks like TensorFlow Lite and Core ML, is becoming increasingly common, offering personalized experiences and enhanced functionalities.

In conclusion, the selection of programming languages and frameworks is a critical aspect of mobile app development, influencing not only the technical capabilities of the app but also the efficiency of the development process and the overall user experience. Java and Kotlin remain pivotal for Android development, while Swift has become the standard for iOS apps. Cross-platform frameworks like React Native and Flutter offer compelling alternatives for projects targeting both Android and iOS, providing efficiency and flexibility. As the mobile app landscape continues to expand and diversify, staying informed about the latest developments in programming languages and frameworks is essential for developers seeking to create innovative, high-quality mobile applications that meet the evolving needs of users.

Agile Development Methodologies

Agile methodologies have revolutionized the mobile app development process, emphasizing flexibility, customer satisfaction, and rapid delivery of functional software. This approach contrasts with traditional waterfall methodologies, which follow a linear, sequential design process. Agile methodologies facilitate adapting to changes in requirements, even late in the development cycle, making them particularly suited to the fast-paced, evolving nature of mobile app development. This section explores the application of agile methodologies in mobile app development, highlighting key principles, practices, and their impact on the development process.

The Agile Manifesto, which puts people and interactions ahead of processes and technologies, functional software ahead of extensive documentation, customer collaboration ahead of contract negotiation, and adapting to change instead of sticking to a plan, is the cornerstone of agile techniques. These values underpin various agile frameworks such as Scrum, Kanban, and Extreme Programming (XP), each offering different strategies and practices tailored to enhance the mobile app development process.

Scrum, one of the most commonly adopted agile frameworks, organizes work into short, iterative cycles known as sprints, commonly lasting two to four weeks. Each sprint takes place with a planning meeting where the development team, along with the product owner and Scrum Master, selects items from a prioritized backlog to focus on. Daily stand-up meetings encourage team communication, while sprint reviews and retrospectives at the end of each cycle facilitate continuous improvement. Scrum's structured approach helps mobile app development teams manage intricate projects by breaking them down into manageable, achievable goals, allowing for regular feedback and adjustments based on user input or changing market demands.

Kanban, another agile methodology, visualizes work, limits work in progress, and enhances flow. In mobile app development, Kanban boards visually track the progress of tasks through different stages, from "To Do" to "Done." This visibility helps teams identify bottlenecks and inefficiencies, promoting a smoother, more continuous workflow. Unlike Scrum, Kanban does not prescribe fixed-length iterations, making it more flexible and adaptable to changes in priorities or scope, which is common in mobile app projects.

Extreme Programming (XP) emphasizes technical excellence and customer satisfaction through frequent releases of functional software. Key practices include pair programming, test-driven development (TDD), continuous integration, and collective code ownership. For mobile app development, XP's focus on quality and responsiveness to customer feedback ensures that the app meets users' needs while maintaining high performance and security standards. The frequent release cycle of XP aligns well with the agile principle of providing working software promptly and frequently, enabling developers to gather user feedback and iterate quickly.

Implementing agile methodologies in mobile app development offers several benefits. Firstly, it enhances flexibility and adaptability, allowing development teams to respond effectively to changing requirements or market conditions. This agility is crucial in the mobile app industry, where user preferences and technological advancements evolve rapidly. Secondly, agile methodologies improve project transparency and communication among stakeholders, including developers, clients, and end-users. Regular meetings, reviews, and the use of visual management tools ensure that everyone involved has a clear understanding of the project's progress and challenges, fostering collaboration and stakeholder engagement.

Moreover, agile methodologies prioritize customer feedback and user experience, ensuring that the developed app aligns with user needs and expectations. Potential problems are found and fixed early through iterative development and frequent testing, lowering the likelihood of expensive rework or project failure. This user-centric strategy improves consumer pleasure and loyalty while raising the possibility of developing a successful app.

However, adopting agile methodologies in mobile app development also presents challenges. These include managing distributed teams, especially in a global development environment, where coordination and communication can be difficult. Ensuring that every team members are properly trained in agile practices and share a common agile mindset is also essential for success. Additionally, the emphasis on rapid development and frequent releases may sometimes compromise the depth of documentation, making it challenging to onboard new team members or maintain the app over time.

To mitigate these challenges, development teams should establish clear communication channels, use collaborative tools, and balance agility and documentation. Regular training sessions and workshops can help teach an agile culture, while practices such as automated testing and continuous integration can enhance efficiency and maintain quality standards.

In conclusion, agile methodologies have become indispensable in mobile app development, offering a flexible, efficient, and user-centered approach to creating high-quality applications. By embracing frameworks like Scrum, Kanban, or Extreme Programming, development teams can navigate the complexities of mobile app projects, adapt to changing requirements, and deliver valuable software promptly. Despite the challenges associated with agile adoption, the benefits of improved flexibility, enhanced communication, and a focus on customer satisfaction make agile methodologies a powerful strategy for mobile app development. Agile approaches will surely be crucial in determining how mobile application development develops in the future as the market for mobile applications expands and changes.

Testing and Debugging Strategies

Testing and debugging are pivotal stages in the mobile app development process, ensuring the delivery of a robust, functional, and user-friendly application. These phases help identify and rectify errors, performance issues, and usability problems, contributing significantly to the app's overall quality and success. This section explores various testing and debugging strategies in mobile app development, highlighting their importance, methodologies, and best practices to ensure the creation of high-quality mobile applications.

The importance of testing and debugging in mobile app development cannot be overstated. In a highly competitive market, users expect apps to perform flawlessly across different devices, operating systems, and network conditions. A single bug or performance issue can lead to negative reviews, decreased user satisfaction, and ultimately, the failure of an app. Therefore, implementing comprehensive testing and debugging strategies is crucial for identifying and fixing issues before the app reaches the end-user, ensuring a positive user experience.

One of the fundamental strategies in mobile app testing is adopting a multi-level testing approach, which includes unit, integration, system, and acceptance testing. Unit testing involves testing individual components or functions of the app for correct behavior. This is usually the first step in the testing process, allowing developers to validate each part of the app in isolation. Integration testing follows, where the interaction between different parts of the app is tested to identify issues in the integration of components. System testing evaluates the app, ensuring it meets the specified requirements and works correctly in all intended environments. Finally, acceptance testing verifies that the app is ready for release, assessing its performance and usability from an end-user's perspective.

Automated testing plays a critical role in efficient and effective testing strategies. Automated tests can be run rapidly and repeatedly, making them ideal for regression testing whenever changes are made to the app. Frameworks such as Selenium, Appium, and Espresso allow for the automation of UI tests, simulating user interactions with the app and verifying that it behaves as expected. Automated testing speeds up the testing process as well as increases its accuracy, reducing the likelihood of human error.

Debugging is an equally critical component of the development process, involving identifying, isolating, and fixing bugs or defects in the app. Effective debugging strategies often begin with clear and consistent logging practices, where developers record detailed information about the app's execution. This can significantly aid in pinpointing the source of errors when they occur. Modern integrated development environments (IDEs) and tools like Android Studio and Xcode provide powerful debugging features, including breakpoints, step-through execution, and variable inspection, which allow developers to closely examine the app's behavior at runtime and identify the root cause of issues.

Performance testing is another vital aspect of the testing strategy, especially for mobile apps, where resources such as memory and battery life are limited. Tools like the Android Profiler and the iOS Instruments app help developers monitor an app's performance in terms of CPU as well as memory usage, and energy consumption. By identifying and optimizing performance bottlenecks, developers can ensure that the app runs smoothly across various devices and conditions.

Usability and accessibility testing are crucial for ensuring that the app gives a positive user experience and is accessible to users with disabilities. This entails testing the app with real users or employing usability testing tools to evaluate the app's design, navigation, and interaction flows. Accessibility testing ensures that the app complies with guidelines like the Web Content Accessibility Guidelines also referred to as WCAG, making it usable for people with various disabilities.

Cross-platform and device testing address the challenge of ensuring that the app functions correctly across different operating systems, screen sizes, and device configurations. Tools like BrowserStack and Sauce Labs allow developers to test mobile apps on an array of devices and operating systems without the need for a physical device lab. This is crucial for identifying platform-specific issues and guaranteeing a consistent user experience irrespective of the user's device.

Finally, continuous integration and continuous delivery (or CI/CD) practices incorporate testing and debugging into the development process, allowing for the automatic building, testing, and deployment of apps. CI/CD pipelines enable developers to quickly identify and address issues, ensuring that only thoroughly tested and stable builds are deployed to users.

In conclusion, testing and debugging are integral to the mobile app development process, ensuring the delivery of high-quality, reliable, and user-friendly applications. Developers can identify and fix issues efficiently by employing a multi-level testing approach, leveraging automated testing, and utilizing modern debugging tools. Performance, usability, and cross-platform testing further ensure that the app delivers a superior user experience across all devices and conditions. Adopting CI/CD practices integrates testing and debugging into the development workflow, facilitating rapid iterations and continuous improvement. By using these strategies, developers can reduce risks, improve app quality, and have more success in the competitive mobile app industry.

CHAPTER V

Monetization Strategies

Freemium vs. Premium Models

The digital landscape of mobile apps has grown exponentially, with developers constantly seeking innovative ways to monetize their creations while providing value to users. Two prevalent models have emerged in this context: freemium and premium. Each model offers a unique approach to app monetization, influencing user engagement, revenue generation, and overall app success. This section explores the distinctions, advantages, and challenges of the freemium and premium models in mobile app development, providing insights into their impact on the market and user experience.

The freemium model is a strategy where the app is offered for free, but certain content, features, and/or services are locked behind a paywall, requiring users to make in-app purchases or subscribe to access the full functionality. This model is designed to lower the barrier to entry, allowing users to download and engage with the app without any initial cost. The rationale is that once users experience the app's value, they will be willing to pay for enhanced features or content, driving revenue for the developers. Freemium models are particularly popular in games, productivity tools, and service-based apps, where the core app provides sufficient utility, but premium features offer significant enhancements or convenience.

On the other hand, the premium model requires users to make an upfront payment to download and use the app.

This model is based on the premise that the app offers exceptional value, quality, or unique features that justify the initial purchase cost. Premium apps often target niche markets or specialized user needs, where the quality and depth of the app's functionality are paramount. This model tends to attract serious users who are more likely to be engaged and loyal, as they have already invested in the app. Developers who choose the premium model must ensure their app stands out in terms of quality, usability, and feature set to persuade users to pay upfront.

Each model has its advantages and challenges. The freemium model's primary advantage is its ability to quickly attract a large user base, as there is no cost barrier to downloading the app. This wide reach can be particularly beneficial for social or network-based apps, where the app's value increases with the number of users. Freemium apps can also generate continuous revenue through in-app purchases and subscriptions, providing a steady income stream that can grow as the user base expands. However, the freemium model faces challenges, including the need to balance free and premium features to ensure that the app remains useful without payment while incentivizing users to upgrade. Additionally, converting free users to paying customers can be difficult, with low conversion rates.

The premium model's advantage lies in its straightforward value proposition: users pay once and get full access to the app's features and content. This can lead to higher initial revenue per user and a user base that is potentially more engaged and committed. Premium apps often have a higher perceived value, which can justify their price and attract users willing to pay for quality. However, the premium model's challenges include a higher barrier to entry, which can limit the initial user base. Developers must invest significantly in marketing to convince users of the app's value before they download it. Additionally, the one-time payment model means developers must find other ways to generate revenue for ongoing development and support.

Choosing between freemium and premium models depends on several factors, including the app's nature, target audience, and long-term monetization strategy. The freemium model may be more suitable for apps that provide a broad range of features or services with potential for incremental upgrades. It allows users to experience the app's core value before deciding to pay for additional features. The premium model might be more appropriate for apps that provide specialized functionality or content with high development costs, ensuring that developers are compensated for their investment from the outset.

In recent years, some developers have explored hybrid models, combining elements of both freemium and premium. For example, an app might offer a free version with basic functionality and a separate, paid premium version with advanced features. Alternatively, developers might provide a free trial period before requiring a purchase or subscription, blending the low barrier to freemium entry with the revenue generation of premium models.

In conclusion, the choice between freemium and premium models in mobile app development involves careful consideration of the app's features, target market, and revenue goals. While the freemium model offers the advantage of a wide potential user base and ongoing revenue opportunities, it challenges developers to convert free users to paying customers. With its upfront payment, the premium model appeals to users willing to invest in quality, though it demands excellence and differentiation to overcome the initial purchase barrier. As the mobile app market evolves, developers must remain adaptable, exploring and possibly combining different monetization strategies to find the most effective approach for their apps. Ultimately, the success of either model depends on creating a compelling, valuable user experience that meets or exceeds user expectations.

In-App Purchases and Subscriptions

In-app purchases and subscriptions have become integral components of the mobile app economy, offering developers a viable revenue stream while providing users with value-added services and features. These monetization strategies have transformed how apps are consumed and paid for, shifting from one-time purchases to ongoing, dynamic interactions between app developers and their users. This section delves into the intricacies of in-app purchases and subscriptions, exploring their benefits, challenges, and impact on the mobile app landscape.

In-app purchases (IAPs) allow users to buy goods or services within an app. These can range from virtual game items like coins, gems, or power-ups to advanced features or additional content in productivity and lifestyle apps. IAPs can be categorized into consumable purchases, which can be used once and need to be bought again (like game currency), and non-consumable, permanent purchases (such as unlocking a full feature set or removing ads). This model allows users to tailor the app experience to their needs and preferences, paying only for what they value.

On the other hand, subscriptions offer users access to a content or services for a recurring fee, commonly on a monthly or annual basis. Subscriptions are commonly used by media and entertainment apps, cloud services, and apps that offer regularly updated content or ongoing services. This model provides a steady revenue stream for developers and encourages them to update and improve their offerings to retain subscribers continually.

The benefits of in-app purchases and subscriptions are manifold. For developers, these models provide an opportunity to offer their apps for free or at a low initial cost, attracting a broader user base. The free or low-cost entry point reduces the barrier to app adoption, allowing users to try the app before committing financially. Once users are engaged and see the value in the app, they are more likely to make purchases or subscribe, generating revenue for the developer. This approach also enables developers to monetize a larger portion of their user base, as opposed to relying solely on upfront purchases, which may deter potential users.

Furthermore, in-app purchases and subscriptions foster a closer relationship between developers and users. By offering additional content or services, developers can continuously engage with their users, gathering feedback and tailoring updates to meet user demands. This ongoing interaction helps build a loyal user base and improve user satisfaction over time.

However, implementing in-app purchases and subscriptions is not without challenges. One of the main issues is balancing monetization with user experience. Overly aggressive monetization strategies, such as gating essential features behind paywalls or inundating users with purchase prompts, can lead to user frustration and app abandonment. Developers must carefully design their monetization approach to ensure that it enhances the app experience rather than detracts from it.

Another challenge is managing in-app purchases and subscriptions' technical and administrative aspects. This includes integrating payment processing systems, handling user subscriptions and cancellations, and complying with the policies of app stores and regulations such as digital tax laws. Developers must also consider the commission fees app stores charges on in-app transactions, which can impact the overall revenue generated.

To mitigate these challenges, developers should focus on providing clear value through their in-app purchases and subscriptions. This could involve offering a compelling free version of the app that demonstrates its value with premium features or content that enhances the user experience. Transparency about the costs and benefits of purchases and subscriptions, along with straightforward management of subscriptions and cancellations, can also help in maintaining user trust and satisfaction.

In addition, developers can leverage analytics to understand user behavior and preferences, tailoring their offerings to meet user needs better. A/B testing different pricing strategies, purchase prompts, and subscription models can provide insights into what resonates with users, allowing developers to optimize their monetization strategy.

In conclusion, in-app purchases and subscriptions represent powerful monetization strategies for mobile apps, offering benefits for both developers and users. While challenges exist, careful planning and a user-centered approach can lead to successful implementation, enhancing app engagement and generating sustainable revenue. As the app economy evolves, in-app purchases and subscriptions will likely remain key components of the monetization mix, driving innovation and growth in the mobile app market.

Advertising and Sponsorships

In mobile app development, monetization strategies play a crucial role in ensuring an app's financial viability and success. Among these strategies, advertising and sponsorships have emerged as effective ways for app developers to generate revenue while providing free or low-cost apps to users. This section explores the intricacies of advertising and sponsorships within mobile app development, examining their benefits, challenges, and the strategies for their effective implementation.

Advertising in mobile apps typically involves displaying third-party ads in various formats, including banner ads, interstitial ads, video ads, and native ads. These ads can be served through ad networks that act as intermediaries between advertisers and developers, automating the process of ad placement and revenue collection. The primary appeal of advertising as a monetization strategy is its ability to offer apps for free to users, thereby increasing the app's accessibility and potential user base. By removing the price barrier, developers can attract a wider audience, which, in turn, becomes attractive to advertisers seeking to reach specific demographics.

Interstitial ads, which appear at natural transition points within an app, and rewarded video ads, which offer users incentives for watching, exemplify how advertising can be integrated to respect the user experience. Native ads, made to match the look and feel of the app, minimize disruption by blending seamlessly with the app's content. When used judiciously, these advertising formats can provide a steady revenue stream while maintaining a positive user experience.

Sponsorships represent another monetization avenue, where a single advertiser or a small group of advertisers exclusively sponsor an app or specific app content. This model allows for deeper integration of the sponsor's brand into the app experience, offering a more cohesive and less intrusive advertising approach. Sponsorships can range from branded content and features within the app to the sponsorship of app updates or events. This strategy generates revenue and can enhance the app's content and features, adding user value while promoting the sponsor's brand.

However, the implementation of advertising and sponsorships within mobile apps is not without challenges. One of the main concerns is the impact on user experience. Excessive or intrusive advertising can lead to user frustration, app abandonment, and negative reviews, harming the app's reputation and long-term success. Developers must carefully balance the need for revenue generation with the importance of maintaining a positive user experience. This involves strategic placement of ads, choosing the right ad formats, and ensuring that sponsored content adds value to the user experience.

Another challenge is maintaining user privacy and trust, especially in light of increasing data protection as well as privacy regulations, including the General Data Protection Regulation in Europe. Advertisers and developers must navigate these regulations carefully, ensuring transparent data collection and usage practices, and providing users with control over their data. Failure to follow with these regulations can result in hefty fines as well as loss of user trust.

To effectively implement advertising and sponsorships, developers should adopt a user-centric approach, prioritizing the user experience in the design and placement of ads. This involves using analytics to understand user behavior and preferences, which can inform the selection of ad formats and the timing of ad placements to minimize disruption. Developers can also explore innovative ad formats and sponsorship models that offer value to users, such as sponsored content that is informative or entertaining, or ads that offer rewards or unlock features within the app.

Moreover, establishing clear partnerships with advertisers and sponsors that align with the app's brand and user demographics is crucial. This alignment ensures that the ads and sponsored content are relevant to the app's users, increasing the likelihood of engagement and positive reception. Transparent communication with users about the role of advertising and sponsorships in supporting the app can also help in maintaining user trust and acceptance.

In conclusion, advertising and sponsorships offer viable monetization strategies for mobile app developers, enabling them to generate revenue while providing free or low-cost apps to a wide audience. When implemented thoughtfully, these strategies can support the app's financial sustainability without compromising the user experience. Developers can leverage advertising and sponsorships effectively by focusing on user-centric design, respecting privacy regulations, and fostering partnerships with relevant advertisers and sponsors. As the mobile app market evolves, adapting these strategies to changing user expectations and technological advancements will be key to their endured success and relevance in app monetization.

Alternative Revenue Streams

In mobile app development's dynamic and competitive landscape, diversifying revenue streams is crucial for sustainability and growth. Beyond the conventional models of in-app purchases, subscriptions, advertising, and sponsorships, developers can explore alternative revenue streams to monetize their applications effectively. This section delves into several innovative and alternative revenue streams in mobile app development, discussing their potential benefits and challenges, and how they can complement traditional monetization strategies.

One alternative revenue stream is the offering of paid premium features or add-ons. This model, often associated with freemium apps, allows users to download and use the core app for free but requires payment for additional premium features or content. Unlike simple in-app purchases, these features significantly enhance the app's functionality or user experience, justifying the additional cost. This strategy not only incentivizes users to invest in the app after they have experienced its value but also caters to varying user needs and willingness to pay, thereby maximizing revenue potential.

Another innovative revenue stream is through partnerships and collaborations. Mobile apps can partner with brands, businesses, or other apps to offer integrated services, co-branded content, or exclusive deals. For instance, a fitness app could collaborate with a sportswear brand to offer exclusive merchandise or personalized training programs. These partnerships provide a direct revenue stream through shared profits or licensing fees and enhance the app's value proposition to users, potentially attracting a wider audience.

Crowdfunding is an emerging revenue stream that involves raising funds for app development or new features directly from users or interested stakeholders. Platforms like Kickstarter and Indiegogo allow developers to pitch their app ideas or planned features to the public, offering rewards or early access in exchange for financial contributions. This model generates initial capital and builds a community of supporters who are invested in the app's success. However, successful crowdfunding campaigns require clear communication, compelling rewards, and transparency about development progress.

Leveraging data analytics and insights offers another avenue for revenue generation. With user consent, developers can collect anonymized data on user behavior, preferences, and interactions within the app. This data can be valuable to market researchers, advertisers, and businesses looking to understand consumer trends or evaluate product demand. Selling data analytics and insights must be approached with caution, prioritizing user privacy and adhering to data protection regulations to maintain trust and compliance.

Content syndication is a strategy where app developers license their content to other media outlets or platforms. For content-rich apps, such as news aggregators, educational platforms, or entertainment apps, syndicating content to third-party websites, apps, or services can generate additional revenue. This model provides financial benefits and increases the app's visibility and reach, potentially driving more users to the original app.

Merchandising is an often-overlooked revenue stream that involves selling branded merchandise related to the app. Popular gaming apps, for instance, can create and sell merchandise like apparel, accessories, or physical versions of in-app items. This strategy works well for apps with a strong brand identity or a loyal user base, offering a tangible way for users to support and engage with the app beyond the digital experience.

Lastly, offering consulting or development services based on the expertise gained through app development can be a lucrative revenue stream. Developers who have successfully navigated the complexities of app development, user engagement, and monetization can offer their expertise to other businesses or developers looking to create or improve their apps. This can include consulting on app design, user experience, monetization strategies, or even custom app development.

Each of these alternative revenue streams presents unique opportunities and challenges. Implementing them requires a deep understanding of the app's user base, market dynamics, and the app's core value proposition. Developers must carefully consider how these strategies align with their overall business goals, user experience, and brand identity. Moreover, transparency with users about monetization strategies is essential to maintain trust and loyalty.

In conclusion, diversifying revenue streams is necessary for mobile apps' long-term sustainability and success. While traditional monetization models provide a solid foundation, exploring alternative revenue streams can enhance profitability, user engagement, and market differentiation. The possibilities are vast, from offering premium features and forming strategic partnerships to leveraging data analytics and exploring merchandising. Successful implementation of these strategies requires creativity, market insight, and a user-centric approach, ensuring monetization efforts add users' value and support the app's overall mission. As the mobile app ecosystem evolves, developers who innovate in their revenue generation strategies will be well-positioned to thrive in this competitive landscape.

CHAPTER VI

Marketing and Promotion

App Store Optimization (ASO)

App Store Optimization (or ASO) is a critical process in the mobile app development ecosystem, designed to enhance an app's visibility in the app stores and enhance its conversion rates. In a marketplace flooded with millions of apps, standing out and capturing the attention of potential users is a formidable challenge. ASO addresses this challenge by employing a range of strategies and techniques to optimize an app's presence in app stores, such as Apple's App Store for iOS devices and Google Play for Android devices. This section explores the various aspects of ASO, its importance, key components, and its impact on mobile app success.

The significance of ASO in mobile app development cannot be overstated. With the overwhelming number of apps available, users often rely on search within app stores to discover new apps. ASO ensures that an app appears prominently in these searches and appears appealing enough to encourage downloads. By optimizing various elements of the app's listing, developers can significantly increase their app's visibility, leading to more organic downloads, higher user engagement, and, ultimately, increased revenue.

One of the fundamental components of ASO is keyword optimization. Keywords are the terms as well as phrases that potential users might utilize to search for apps within the app stores. Including relevant keywords in the app's title, subtitle, and description can dramatically improve the app's search rankings. Conducting thorough keyword research to have a knowledge of the most relevant terms with a high search volume but low competition is crucial. Regularly updating and refining the app's keywords based on changing trends and user behavior can help maintain high visibility.

Another key aspect of ASO is optimizing the app's title and description. The title should be catchy and memorable and include the most important keyword. The description should provide a clear and compelling overview of what the app does, its key features, and why it stands out from competitors. Well-crafted titles and descriptions improve search visibility and increase the likelihood of conversion by convincing users of the app's value.

Visual elements play a significant role in ASO. The app's icon, screenshots, and preview videos are the first visual cues that potential users encounter. These elements should be visually appealing, convey the app's purpose at a glance, and highlight its key features and benefits. High-quality, engaging visuals can significantly increase the app's click-through rate (CTR) from search results and its conversion rate from views to downloads.

User reviews and ratings are integral to ASO. High ratings and positive reviews enhance the app's credibility and can significantly affect its search rankings and user perception. Encouraging satisfied users to leave reviews and resolving negative feedback quickly can help maintain a positive rating. Implementing features within the app to facilitate easy review submissions can also increase the volume of positive feedback.

Localization is another critical consideration in ASO. Tailoring the app's listing for different languages and regions can tap into global markets more effectively. Localization involves translating the app's title, description, keywords, and other metadata into the languages of the target markets. It also includes adapting the visual elements to reflect cultural preferences. Localization can dramatically increase an app's reach and appeal to a broader audience.

Regular monitoring and analysis are crucial for effective ASO. Developers should use analytics tools to track their app's performance in the app stores, including its rankings, downloads, and conversion rates. Analyzing this data allows developers to understand which ASO strategies are working and which areas need improvement. Continuous testing and optimization based on data-driven insights can help maintain and improve the app's visibility and conversion rates over time.

In conclusion, App Store Optimization is essential to mobile app development and marketing. It encompasses a range of strategies to enhance an app's visibility in app stores and improve its conversion rates. Developers can significantly increase their app's organic downloads and success by optimizing keywords, titles, descriptions, and visual elements and encouraging positive reviews. Localization and regular monitoring and analysis further refine ASO efforts, ensuring the app effectively reaches its target audience. As the mobile app market grows and evolves, ASO remains a dynamic and critical process for developers aiming to stand out in a crowded marketplace.

Social Media Marketing

In the quickly evolving digital landscape, social media marketing has become a crucial element in the promotion and success of mobile apps. This dynamic and interactive marketing strategy leverages the power of social media platforms to improve visibility, engage potential users, and drive app downloads. Integrating social media marketing in mobile app development encompasses a strategic approach to reaching target audiences, fostering community engagement, and building brand loyalty. This section delves into the importance of social media marketing in mobile app development, outlining its benefits, strategies, and impact on the overall success of mobile applications.

It is impossible to exaggerate the significance of social media marketing for the promotion of mobile apps. App developers have access to an array of people on social media, with billions of users on sites like Facebook, Instagram, LinkedIn, and Twitter. Social media is an essential component of the app marketing toolset because these platforms present distinctive chances to communicate, advertise, and publish material that is specifically tailored to potential customers. By leveraging social media, developers can create buzz around their app, generate interest, and ultimately drive downloads and user engagement.

The capacity of social media marketing to accurately target particular groups is one of its main advantages. Social media companies gather a lot of information on their users, such as demographics, interests, and usage patterns. This data enables developers to tailor their marketing efforts to reach their ideal audience with relevant content and messaging. Whether it's a productivity app aimed at professionals or a gaming app designed for teenagers, social media marketing allows for targeted campaigns that resonate with the intended user base.

Another advantage is the potential for viral marketing. Social media's interconnected nature means that content can quickly spread across networks, reaching a broad audience quickly. Developers can encourage users to recommend their app with friends and followers by producing shareable content, including interesting movies, educational infographics, or interactive challenges. This will naturally increase the reach of the developer's marketing campaign. Because consumers are more likely to believe suggestions from their social network, viral marketing increases app visibility and gives credibility.

Engagement is at the heart of social media marketing. Unlike traditional advertising, which is often one-way, social media allows for two-way interactions between the app developers and potential or current users. Developers can use social media platforms to respond to queries, gather feedback, and engage in conversations, building a community around their app. This direct engagement encourages a sense of connection and loyalty among users, which is invaluable for retaining users and encouraging positive reviews and word-of-mouth recommendations.

Social media marketing also offers flexibility and adaptability. The digital nature of social media allows developers to quickly change their marketing strategies based on performance metrics, user feedback, and changing trends. A/B testing different messages, visuals, and calls to action can help determine the most effective tactics for driving app downloads and engagement. Moreover, social media platforms frequently introduce new features, such as Instagram Stories or Twitter Polls, providing fresh avenues for creative marketing campaigns.

However, successful social media marketing needs a strategic approach. Developers must first identify the most suitable platforms for their target audience. For example, LinkedIn might be more effective for B2B apps, while Instagram and TikTok could be better suited for consumer-focused apps targeting younger audiences. Developing a content strategy that is in line with the app's brand voice and user interests is crucial. Content should be varied, engaging, and provide value, whether it's through tips, entertainment, or insights related to the app's niche.

Influencer marketing has appeared as a potent strategy within social media marketing. Collaborating with influencers with a strong following in the app's target market can significantly increase visibility and credibility. Influencers can provide authentic endorsements, share their experiences with the app, and motivate their followers to download and try the app. This approach leverages influencers' trust and rapport with their audience, translating into higher engagement and conversion rates.

In conclusion, social media marketing is pivotal in successfully promoting mobile apps. By leveraging social media platforms' vast reach, targeting capabilities, and interactive nature, developers can enhance visibility, engage with potential users, and drive app downloads. Understanding the target market, producing interesting and timely content, and building a community around the app all depend on effective social media marketing. Mobile app developers can accomplish short-term marketing objectives and establish a solid basis for sustained success and customer loyalty in the competitive app industry by implementing a planned approach to social network marketing.

Influencer Partnerships

In the contemporary mobile app development landscape, influencer partnerships have emerged as a powerful and innovative marketing strategy. Leveraging the reach and credibility of influencers across social media platforms, developers can significantly enhance their mobile apps' visibility, user engagement, and overall success. This section delves into the nuances of influencer partnerships in mobile app development, exploring the rationale behind their effectiveness, the process of establishing these partnerships, and the potential benefits and challenges they present.

The genesis of influencer partnerships in mobile app development is rooted in the evolving dynamics of digital marketing and consumer behavior. In an age where traditional advertising often falls short of capturing the audience's attention, influencers offer a personal and authentic channel to reach potential users. Influencers, with their dedicated followers and expertise in content creation, can introduce an app to a vast audience in a way that feels organic and trustworthy. This marketing method is particularly effective because it leverages the trust that influencers have built with their audience, translating this trust into a compelling endorsement for the app.

The effectiveness of influencer partnerships hinges on the influencer's relevance to the app's target audience and the authenticity of the partnership. For an influencer partnership to be successful, the influencer's audience must align with the app's intended user base. This alignment ensures that the app is promoted to individuals most likely to be interested in its features and benefits. Moreover, the authenticity of the influencer's endorsement plays a vital role in the partnership's success. Audiences are adept at discerning genuine recommendations from forced advertisements, and an authentic endorsement can significantly influence the audience's perception and willingness to download and engage with the app.

Establishing influencer partnerships involves a strategic process that begins with identifying the right influencers. This identification process entails analyzing the influencer's audience demographics, engagement rates, and content relevance to ensure a good fit with the app's marketing objectives. Once potential influencers are identified, developers or marketers must submit a proposal outlining the partnership's terms, including expectations, deliverables, and compensation. Successful partnerships often involve a collaborative approach, where influencers are given creative freedom to present the app in a way that resonates with their audience while aligning with the app's branding and messaging goals.

The benefits of influencer partnerships are manifold. Firstly, they offer targeted access to potential users, with influencers acting as a bridge between the app and a highly engaged audience. Secondly, influencer endorsements can significantly enhance the app's credibility and desirability, as recommendations from trusted influencers carry weight and can influence consumer behavior. Thirdly, influencer content can provide valuable exposure and generate buzz, creating a viral effect that amplifies the app's visibility beyond the influencer's direct followers. This exposure can lead to increased downloads, higher app store rankings, and, ultimately, greater revenue potential for the app. However,

navigating influencer partnerships also presents challenges. One of the primary challenges is ensuring the alignment of values and expectations between the influencer and the app developers. Misalignments can lead to ineffective campaigns or potentially damage the app's reputation. Additionally, measuring the return on investment (or ROI) of influencer partnerships can be complex, as the impact of these partnerships extends beyond direct app downloads to include brand awareness and user engagement metrics. Developers must employ comprehensive tracking and analytics to assess influencer partnerships' effectiveness accurately.

To maximize the benefits as well as mitigate the challenges of influencer partnerships, developers should adopt best practices such as conducting thorough research to identify the most suitable influencers, establishing clear and transparent communication regarding expectations and compensation, and fostering long-term relationships with influencers to build sustained advocacy for the app. Integrating influencer partnerships into a broader marketing strategy is crucial, ensuring a cohesive and multifaceted approach to app promotion.

In conclusion, influencer partnerships represent a dynamic and impactful mobile app development and marketing strategy. By leveraging influencers' reach, credibility, and content creation skills, developers can effectively promote their apps to targeted audiences, enhance brand credibility, and drive user engagement and downloads. While the process involves careful planning, negotiation, and monitoring, the potential rewards of influencer partnerships in terms of visibility and growth are substantial. As the digital landscape evolves, influencer partnerships will undoubtedly remain a key component of successful mobile app marketing strategies, offering a unique blend of authenticity, engagement, and targeted reach.

Public Relations and Press Coverage

Public relations (PR) and press coverage have become indispensable tools in the arsenal of mobile app development and marketing strategies. In an era where the digital marketplace is saturated with countless applications, standing out and capturing the attention of potential users and stakeholders require more than just a well-designed app. Effective PR and press coverage can elevate an app's profile, build its brand, and significantly impact its success. This section explores the roles of public relations and press coverage in mobile app development, highlighting their benefits, strategies for success, and the challenges developers might face in executing effective PR campaigns.

The significance of PR and press coverage in mobile app development lies in their ability to generate awareness and credibility. Unlike traditional advertising, which directly promotes a product or service, PR focuses on building positive relationships and perceptions among the app's target audience through media and public engagement. As a PR component, press coverage involves getting journalists, bloggers, and influencers to write or talk about the app, providing an endorsement that can be more persuasive and far-reaching than advertising alone. This third-party validation enhances the app's visibility and lends it credibility, which is crucial in a competitive market.

One of the primary benefits of PR and press coverage is the potential for broad exposure. A well-placed article in a popular tech blog, a mention by a respected industry influencer, or a feature in a mainstream media outlet can quickly introduce the app to a vast audience. This exposure is particularly valuable for new apps or developers with limited marketing budgets, as it provides a cost-effective way to reach potential users. Furthermore, press coverage can be targeted to reach specific demographics or interest groups, ensuring that the message reaches the most relevant audience.

Another advantage is the establishment and reinforcement of the app's brand. Effective PR helps craft and communicate the app's unique value proposition, mission, and identity. Developers can shape public perception through consistent messaging and strategic media engagement, creating a strong brand that resonates with users and distinguishes the app from competitors. This branding effort supports long-term growth and user loyalty and can even attract investment and partnerships by positioning the app as a leader in its category.

To achieve successful PR and press coverage, developers must employ strategic planning and execution. This process begins with identifying the app's key messages and unique selling points. What makes the app different? How does it benefit users? Answering these questions can help developers articulate a compelling narrative that captures the interest of the media and the public. Next, identifying the right media outlets and influencers who align with the app's target audience and thematic focus is crucial. Personalized pitches highlighting the app's relevance to the outlet's readership or the influencer's followers are more likely to result in coverage.

Building relationships with journalists, bloggers, and influencers is also critical. Engaging with these individuals through social media, networking events, and direct outreach can foster connections that facilitate future coverage. Offering exclusive previews, demos, or interviews can provide media professionals with valuable content for their audiences, making it a mutually beneficial relationship.

However, navigating the world of PR and press coverage presents challenges. One of the main hurdles is capturing the media's attention in a crowded market. Developers must ensure their pitches stand out by being newsworthy, timely, and relevant. Additionally, managing media relations requires time, effort, and sometimes expertise that developers may not have, necessitating hiring PR professionals or agencies. Another challenge is measuring the impact of PR efforts. While tools and metrics can track reach and engagement, quantifying the direct effect on app downloads and revenue can be complex.

Despite these challenges, the potential rewards of effective PR and press coverage make it a worthwhile endeavor for mobile app developers. By increasing visibility, building credibility, and establishing a strong brand, PR and press coverage can significantly contribute to an app's success. Developers can navigate the complexities of PR by staying authentic, focusing on building relationships, and continuously refining their strategies based on outcomes and feedback.

In conclusion, public relations and press coverage are critical to a comprehensive mobile app development strategy. They offer a path to increased visibility, credibility, and brand strength in a competitive digital marketplace. While achieving effective PR requires strategic planning, relationship building, and sometimes overcoming challenges, the potential benefits in terms of user engagement and app success are substantial. As the app ecosystem continues to evolve, leveraging the power of PR and press coverage will remain a vital strategy for developers looking to make a lasting impact.

CHAPTER VII

Launching Your App

Pre-launch Strategies

Pre-launch strategies in mobile app development are critical to successfully introducing and adopting an app. These strategies encompass a range of activities undertaken before the app is officially available on app stores, aiming to build anticipation, engage potential users, and ensure a smooth rollout. This section explores the significance of pre-launch strategies, their key components, and their impact on a mobile app's success trajectory.

The importance of pre-launch strategies cannot be overstated. They are the foundation for the app's market entry, creating the initial buzz and user interest necessary for a successful launch. By effectively implementing pre-launch strategies, developers can significantly increase their app's visibility, attract an initial user base, and gather valuable feedback, all of which contribute to the app's long-term success. Furthermore, these strategies enable developers to refine their marketing messages, identify and address potential issues, and build a community around the app even before it becomes available.

Market research and target audience identification are among the first steps in a successful pre-launch strategy. Understanding who the app is for, and their needs, preferences, and behaviors is crucial in tailoring the app's features, design, and marketing efforts. This research informs all subsequent pre-launch activities, ensuring they are focused and effective. Developers can use surveys, focus groups, and competitor analysis to obtain insights into the target market and position their app accordingly.

Building a landing page or a pre-launch website is another essential component of pre-launch strategies. This online presence is a central hub for information about the app, offering an overview of its features, benefits, and unique selling points. A well-designed landing page can generate interest, capture email addresses or pre-registrations, and begin building a relationship with potential users. By including a call-to-action, such as signing up for a newsletter or notification of the app's release, developers can start creating a database of interested users who can be engaged through email marketing campaigns.

Social media is pivotal in pre-launch strategies, offering platforms to build and engage a community around the app. Developers can use social media to share updates, teasers, and behind-the-scenes content related to the app's development, fostering anticipation and excitement. Engaging with potential users through comments, polls, and discussions can also provide valuable feedback and create a sense of involvement and investment in the app's success. Selecting the right platforms based on where the target audience is most active is crucial to maximizing the impact of social media efforts.

Content marketing is another effective pre-launch strategy. By producing and disseminating insightful information pertaining to the app's theme or sector, developers can draw in and hold the interest of potential users. This information can be posted on the app's website, social network pages, and other pertinent channels. It can also take the shape of blog entries, videos, infographics, and podcasts. In addition to improving pre-launch sign-ups and brand recognition, content marketing increases traffic to the app's landing page.

Pre-launch tactics must include beta testing since it enables developers to get user feedback, find issues, and evaluate the general usability of the program. By asking a small number of people to test the app, you may learn more about how actual users interact with it and identify areas that need work. Early evaluations and testimonials from beta testers can also be added to marketing materials to establish credibility and trust.

Influencer partnerships can amplify pre-launch efforts significantly. Collaborating with influencers who have a strong following among the target audience can increase visibility and lend credibility to the app. Influencers can share their experiences with the app's beta version, create buzz, and drive their followers to the app's landing page or sign-up list. Selecting influencers whose values and audience align with the app's target market is key to the effectiveness of this strategy.

Lastly, a comprehensive launch plan is crucial to capitalize on the momentum built during the pre-launch phase. This plan should detail the specific activities, timelines, and channels for the official launch, ensuring the app's coordinated and impactful introduction to the market. The launch plan should also include strategies for continued engagement, user acquisition, and retention post-launch.

In conclusion, pre-launch strategies are integral to successfully introducing a mobile app. By conducting thorough market research, building a landing page, leveraging social media and content marketing, conducting beta testing, partnering with influencers, and developing a comprehensive launch plan, developers can create a strong foundation for their app's success. These strategies generate anticipation and early interest and provide valuable feedback and insights that can enhance the app's quality and user experience. As the mobile app market grows and evolves, effective pre-launch strategies will remain critical to achieving visibility, engagement, and long-term success in this competitive space.

App Store Submission Process

The App Store submission process is a critical final step in mobile app development, involving the review and approval of apps by platform-specific app stores, such as Apple's App Store for iOS apps and Google Play for Android apps. This process is designed to ensure that apps meet specific quality, functionality, and security standards before they become available to users. Navigating the App Store submission process successfully requires a thorough understanding of each platform's guidelines, meticulous preparation, and strategic planning. This section explores the App Store submission process, highlighting the key steps, requirements, and best practices for developers aiming to launch their apps smoothly and efficiently.

Understanding the specific guidelines and requirements of the target app store is the first and most crucial step in the submission process. Apple's App Store and Google Play have detailed guidelines covering app design, functionality, content, privacy, and security. Apple, known for its stringent review process, requires apps to offer valuable content, provide a high-quality user experience, and adhere to strict privacy standards. Google Play also emphasizes the importance of app quality and user privacy but tends to have a more streamlined approval process. Familiarizing oneself with these guidelines early in the development process can help avoid common pitfalls that lead to submission rejections.

Preparing the app for submission involves several key steps, starting with thorough testing to ensure the app is free of bugs, crashes, and performance issues. Beta testing with a group of end-users can provide valuable feedback and help identify any remaining issues. Additionally, developers must ensure that the app complies with all legal requirements, including copyright laws, data protection regulations, and age rating guidelines. Preparing a comprehensive set of materials to accompany the app submission is also essential. This includes crafting a compelling app description, selecting keywords for App Store optimization (ASO), creating high-quality screenshots and preview videos, and setting up metadata such as the app's category, price, and privacy policy.

Creating an account with the app store's developer program is a prerequisite for submission. For Apple's App Store, this involves enrolling in the Apple Developer Program, which requires an annual fee. Google Play requires developers to set up a Google Play Developer account and also pay a one-time registration fee. These accounts provide access to the respective app store's developer tools, resources, and analytics, enabling developers to manage their app submissions and monitor performance post-launch.

The submission process typically involves filling out a form through the app store's developer console, uploading the app package, and submitting the prepared materials and metadata. For iOS apps, developers use Xcode, Apple's integrated development environment, to archive the app and upload it to App Store Connect, where they can manage the submission process. Google Play developers upload their app's APK or App Bundle files through the Google Play Console. Once submitted, the app undergoes a review process, where app store reviewers assess it against the store's guidelines and criteria.

The review times can vary, with Apple's App Store generally taking a few days to a week and Google Play often completing reviews more quickly. During this time, developers may receive feedback or requests for additional information from the reviewers. Addressing these requests promptly and accurately is crucial to advancing the review process. If the app is rejected, developers should carefully review the feedback, make the necessary adjustments, and resubmit the app for review.

Upon approval, the app becomes available on the app store, marking the beginning of its public life. However, the submission process does not end with approval. Developers should actively monitor the app's performance, user reviews, and ratings, using this feedback to inform future updates and improvements. Both app stores offer mechanisms for updating apps, requiring developers to submit new versions through a similar review process.

Successfully navigating the app store submission process needs careful attention to detail, adherence to app store guidelines, and a proactive approach to addressing feedback and rejections. Best practices for a smooth submission process include starting the preparation early, conducting thorough testing, engaging in ASO, and staying informed about changes to app store policies and guidelines.

In conclusion, the app store submission process is vital in bringing a mobile app to market. By understanding the requirements of the target app store, preparing meticulously, and responding constructively to feedback, developers can increase their chances of a successful submission. Although the process can be challenging and sometimes frustrating, it serves as a crucial quality control mechanism, ensuring that only apps meeting specific standards reach users. With strategic planning and execution, developers can navigate the app store submission process effectively, laying the foundation for their app's success in the competitive mobile app marketplace.

Post-launch Monitoring and Optimization

The journey of mobile app development does not conclude with its launch; in fact, the launch signifies the beginning of a crucial phase known as post-launch monitoring and optimization. This phase is pivotal for the sustained success and growth of the app, requiring developers to engage in continuous analysis, feedback collection, and iterative improvements. This section explores the significance of post-launch monitoring and optimization in mobile app development, detailing the processes involved, the tools utilized, and the strategies for enhancing app performance and user satisfaction over time.

Post-launch monitoring and optimization are fundamental for several reasons. Firstly, they enable developers to identify and rectify any technical issues that might not have been evident during the testing phases, such as bugs, crashes, or performance problems in specific devices or operating systems. Secondly, this phase allows for gathering user feedback, which is invaluable for understanding user satisfaction, preferences, and pain points. Thirdly, monitoring user interaction with the app provides insights into usage patterns, feature popularity, and potential areas for improvement or expansion. Collectively, these insights guide the iterative development process, ensuring the app evolves in alignment with user needs and market demands.

The process of post-launch monitoring begins with implementing analytics tools within the app. Tools such as Google Analytics for Firebase, Flurry Analytics, or Mixpanel offer comprehensive insights into user behavior, engagement metrics, retention rates, and conversion statistics. These tools allow developers to track key performance indicators (or KPIs), such as daily active users (DAU), session length, and in-app purchase revenue, providing a quantitative basis for evaluating the app's performance.

In parallel to analytics, collecting user feedback is essential to post-launch optimization. Feedback can be obtained through numerous channels, including in-app surveys, app store reviews, social media, and customer support inquiries. This qualitative feedback complements the quantitative data from analytics, offering a holistic view of the user experience. Developers should actively encourage users to share their thoughts and suggestions, demonstrating a commitment to user satisfaction and continuous improvement.

Developers must prioritize and implement optimizations and updates based on the insights obtained from analytics and user feedback. This might involve fixing bugs and technical issues, refining existing features for better usability, adding new content or functionalities based on user demand, or enhancing the app's performance and efficiency. Each update should be strategically planned, with clear objectives and metrics for success, to ensure it contributes positively to the app's overall performance and user experience.

Another crucial aspect of post-launch optimization is A/B testing, which entails comparing two versions of an app feature or interface to determine which performs better regarding user engagement or conversion. A/B testing allows developers to make data-driven decisions, minimizing the risks of major changes or new features. By systematically testing and analyzing the results, developers can incrementally improve the app's appeal and usability.

Marketing and user acquisition efforts also play a significant role in post-launch optimization. Even the most well-designed as well as functional app can fail to achieve its potential without effective promotion. Developers should continue marketing activities post-launch, leveraging the initial user base and app store visibility to attract new users. This might include running advertising campaigns, engaging in content marketing, or partnering with influencers. Optimizing the app store listing based on user feedback and performance metrics can improve its visibility and attractiveness to potential users.

Monitoring the competitive landscape is equally vital in the post-launch phase. Developers should monitor competing apps, industry trends, and technological advancements to ensure their apps remain competitive and relevant. This might involve adopting new technologies, adjusting the app's value proposition, or pivoting the app's focus in response to market shifts. Post-

launch monitoring and optimization challenges include managing the volume of data and feedback, prioritizing development efforts, and maintaining user engagement over time. Developers must be strategic in their approach, focusing on changes that significantly impact user satisfaction and business objectives. Additionally, balancing the need for rapid iteration with the risk of overwhelming users with frequent updates requires careful consideration.

In conclusion, post-launch monitoring and optimization are critical for the long-term success of mobile apps. Developers can enhance app performance, address user needs, and respond to market dynamics by engaging in continuous analysis, feedback collection, and iterative improvements. This proactive and data-driven approach ensures the app remains competitive, relevant, and valuable to users, driving sustained growth and success in the ever-evolving mobile app landscape.

CHAPTER VIII

User Engagement and Retention

Building a Community Around Your App

Building a community around your app is a strategic approach that transcends mere app development, aiming to create a loyal user base engaged in continuous interaction with your app and with each other. This community-building endeavor fosters a sense of belonging among users and significantly contributes to the app's growth, sustainability, and innovation. This section delves into the significance of community building in app development, outlines strategies for cultivating such a community, and discusses the benefits and challenges associated with this process.

The importance of building a community around your app cannot be overstated. In an increasingly competitive digital landscape, where users are bombarded with myriad app choices, a strong community can be the differentiating factor that propels an app to sustained success. A community provides a platform for users to share experiences, offer feedback, and contribute ideas, thereby enhancing user engagement and loyalty. Moreover, it is a valuable source of user-generated content and organic marketing, as community members are likely to advocate for the app within their networks. To

build a community around an app, developers must first clearly know their target audience and what motivates them to engage with the app. This understanding forms the basis for creating a community that resonates with the users' interests, needs, and preferences. Following this, developers should identify the most suitable platforms for community interaction, which could range from social media groups and forums to in-app community features. The choice of platform should align with where the target audience is most active and comfortable engaging.

Creating valuable as well as engaging content is crucial for fostering community interaction. This could include tips and tricks, behind-the-scenes insights, user stories, or updates about the app. The content should encourage participation, prompting users to share their experiences, ask questions, as well as communicate with each other. Regularly scheduling events, challenges, or competitions can also stimulate community engagement, providing opportunities for users to connect over shared interests and activities related to the app.

Listening to and acting on community feedback is another key strategy in community building. Users who feel heard and see their input reflected in app updates and improvements are more likely to remain engaged and loyal. This feedback loop enhances the app's features and usability and strengthens the community's sense of ownership and investment in the app's success.

Incentivizing participation can further energize the community. Rewards, recognition, and exclusive benefits for active community members can encourage more users to participate and contribute. Whether it's through a points system, badges, special access to new features, or public acknowledgment, incentives can motivate users to become more involved in the community.

However, building and maintaining an app community presents several challenges. One of the primary challenges is ensuring sustained engagement. As the app's novelty or community wanes, users may become less active, necessitating continuous efforts to introduce fresh content, events, and incentives to rekindle interest.

Managing the community also requires significant time and resources, from moderating discussions to responding to feedback and organizing events. Developers must be prepared to invest in community management to maintain a positive and active environment.

Moreover, handling negative feedback or conflicts within the community requires tact and diplomacy. Establishing clear community guidelines and dealing with issues promptly and fairly can help mitigate conflicts and maintain a supportive community atmosphere. Developers must balance fostering open dialogue and ensuring the community remains a positive space for all members.

Despite these challenges, the advantages of building a community around your app are manifold. A vibrant community enhances user retention and loyalty and drives organic growth through word-of-mouth marketing. Community feedback and ideas can be invaluable for app improvement and innovation, helping developers stay aligned with user needs and preferences. Furthermore, a strong community can attract partnerships, sponsorships, and other opportunities, contributing to the app's financial sustainability.

In conclusion, building a community around your app is a strategic endeavor that extends beyond app development, aiming to create an engaged and loyal user base. By understanding the target audience, developing an engaging content, listening to feedback, and incentivizing participation, developers can cultivate a vibrant community that contributes to the app's growth and success. Despite the challenges, the benefits of a supportive and active community are undeniable, offering a competitive edge in the crowded app marketplace. As such, community building should be an integral part of any app development and marketing strategy, driving user engagement, loyalty, and innovation.

Push Notifications and In-App Messaging

In the digital age, where mobile apps are integral to daily life, engaging users and maintaining their interest is a constant challenge for developers. Push notifications and in-app messaging have emerged as vital tools in this endeavor, offering direct communication with users. These features not only improve user engagement but also significantly contribute to the retention and monetization strategies of mobile apps. This section explores the roles, benefits, and strategic implementation of push notifications and in-app messaging in mobile app development.

Push notifications are messages that show up on a user's mobile device, alerting them to updates, promotions, or other relevant information from an app, even when the app is not actively in use. In contrast, in-app messaging refers to messages that users receive while they are actively using the app, providing timely information or offers related to their in-app activities. Both push notifications and in-app messaging serve to keep users informed, engaged, and connected with the app, but they do so in different contexts and with different user engagement strategies in mind.

The significance of push notifications and in-app messaging lies in their capacity to deliver timely and personalized content directly to users. In a landscape crowded with apps vying for attention, these communication tools help apps stand out and remind users of their value. Whether it's notifying users about a new feature, a special offer, or simply nudging them to complete an action, push notifications and in-app messages can significantly increase user engagement and drive app usage.

One of the major benefits of push notifications and in-app messaging is the ability to deliver personalized content. By leveraging user data and behavior analytics, developers can tailor messages to fit individual user preferences, interests, and usage patterns. This personalization enhances the relevance of the messages, increasing the likelihood of user engagement and positive response. For example, a fitness app might send a push notification to remind users about their workout schedule or congratulate them on reaching a milestone, encouraging continued app usage.

Another advantage is the potential for increasing user retention. Regular, well-crafted communication keeps the app top-of-mind for users, reducing the chances of app abandonment. Notifications and messages that provide genuine value, such as useful tips, reminders, or exclusive offers, can reinforce the app's utility and strengthen user loyalty. Additionally, these tools can be used to re-engage users who have not used the app for a while, enticing them back with updates or special promotions.

Implementing push notifications and in-app messaging effectively requires a strategic approach. It is crucial to strike a balance between keeping users informed and avoiding overwhelming them with excessive messaging. Developers must carefully consider messages' frequency, timing, and content to ensure they enhance the user experience rather than detract from it. Opt-in options and user controls for notifications can help respect user preferences and reduce the risk of annoyance or uninstalls.

Segmentation and targeting are also essential for maximizing the impact of push notifications and in-app messages. By dividing the user base into segments based on behavior, demographics, or preferences, developers can ensure that messages are highly targeted and relevant. Advanced targeting can lead to higher engagement rates, as users receive content that is specifically relevant to their interests and needs.

However, the use of push notifications and in-app messaging comes with challenges. Users may perceive these communications as intrusive or spammy if not executed with sensitivity and relevance. There is also the risk of notification fatigue, where users become desensitized to messages due to overuse, leading to decreased effectiveness. Furthermore, navigating the technical aspects of implementing these features, such as managing permissions and optimizing delivery across different devices and operating systems, requires technical expertise and resources.

Despite these challenges, the benefits of integrating push notifications and in-app messaging into mobile app development strategies are significant. These tools can enhance user engagement, increase retention, and drive app usage when used thoughtfully. They offer a direct channel to communicate with users, providing opportunities to deliver personalized, timely, and valuable content that enriches the user experience.

In conclusion, push notifications and in-app messaging are powerful tools in the arsenal of mobile app developers, enabling them to maintain an ongoing dialogue with users. By delivering personalized and relevant content, these features can significantly enhance user engagement, retention, and app success. However, their effectiveness depends on a strategic and user-centric approach to implementation, emphasizing the importance of relevance, timing, and user control. As mobile apps continue to evolve, the role of push notifications and in-app messaging in creating meaningful and lasting user engagement will undoubtedly grow, underscoring their importance in the competitive landscape of mobile app development.

Feedback Loops and Continuous Improvement

In the dynamic world of mobile app development, the concept of feedback loops and continuous improvement has become a cornerstone for success. This approach ensures that apps evolve in response to user needs and preferences and fosters a culture of perpetual enhancement and adaptation. Integrating feedback loops into the development process allows app creators to refine their offerings, fix issues promptly, and introduce innovations that keep users engaged over time. This section explores the significance of feedback loops and continuous improvement in mobile app development, highlighting their benefits, implementation strategies, and impact on mobile applications' longevity and success.

Feedback loops refer to the systematic process of gathering, analyzing, and acting upon feedback from various stakeholders, most importantly, the users. This feedback can range from bug reports and feature requests to suggestions for improvement and general user experience insights. The essence of feedback loops is in their cyclicity—feedback is continuously solicited, evaluated, and used to make informed decisions that guide the development of subsequent app versions. This iterative process guarantees that the app remains relevant, user-friendly, and ahead of the competition.

The importance of integrating feedback loops and continuous improvement into mobile app development cannot be overstated. In today's fast-paced digital environment, user expectations are ever-evolving, and technological advancements occur at a breakneck pace. An app that remains static, ignoring user feedback and new trends, is likely to become obsolete quickly. By embracing feedback loops, developers can ensure their apps adapt to changing user needs, incorporate new technologies, and address any issues hindering user satisfaction.

One of the primary benefits of feedback loops is the ability to identify and rectify problems swiftly. Whether it's a minor bug affecting the user interface or a significant flaw impacting app functionality, feedback from users provides direct insight into issues that need immediate attention. Addressing these problems promptly improves the app's performance and signals to users that their input is valued, enhancing their sense of investment in the app's success.

Moreover, feedback loops facilitate the prioritization of feature development and enhancements. By analyzing feedback, developers can discern which potential features are most desired by users, which improvements could enhance user experience, and which areas of the app are most problematic. This insight allows for more strategic resource allocation, ensuring that development efforts focus on areas that will significantly impact user satisfaction and engagement.

Implementing effective feedback loops involves several key strategies. Firstly, developers must establish reliable channels for collecting feedback. This can include in-app feedback mechanisms, email support, user forums, social media interactions, and app store reviews. Offering multiple avenues for feedback ensures that users can easily communicate their thoughts and suggestions, increasing the volume and diversity of feedback received.

Secondly, developers should employ tools and systems for organizing and analyzing feedback. Given the potentially vast amount of data collected, it's crucial to have processes in place to categorize feedback, identify common themes, and prioritize issues for resolution. Analytics tools, customer relationship management (or CRM) systems, and project management software can help in this process, helping developers to manage feedback efficiently and make data-driven decisions.

Thirdly, transparency with users about how their feedback is being used is essential for maintaining trust and engagement. Developers can communicate updates, bug fixes, and new features through app release notes, blog posts, or direct messages to users. Acknowledging user contributions fosters a positive community around the app and encourages ongoing feedback.

However, implementing feedback loops and continuous improvement is not without challenges. Managing user expectations, particularly regarding feature requests that are not feasible or outside the app's scope, requires clear communication and sometimes difficult decisions. Additionally, the continuous iteration of the app based on feedback can strain resources and necessitate a flexible development approach to accommodate ongoing changes.

Despite these challenges, the advantages of embracing feedback loops and continuous improvement are substantial. This approach drives innovation, enhances user satisfaction, and ultimately contributes to the app's long-term success. By staying responsive to user feedback and committed to continuous improvement, developers can create apps that not only meet but it exceed user expectations, securing their place in the competitive landscape of mobile applications.

In conclusion, feedback loops and continuous improvement are essential for mobile app development. They enable developers to create dynamic, user-centric apps that evolve in response to feedback, technological advancements, and changing market conditions. Through effective implementation of feedback loops, developers can ensure their apps remain relevant, functional, and appealing to users, fostering a cycle of continuous engagement and improvement. This approach improves the user experience as well as contributes to the sustainability and success of mobile apps in a rapidly evolving digital ecosystem.

CHAPTER IX

Scaling Your App Business

Scaling Infrastructure and Resources

Scaling infrastructure and resources in mobile app development is crucial for developers as well as businesses aiming to achieve long-term success and handle growth efficiently. As apps gain popularity and user bases expand, the underlying infrastructure must support increased loads, maintain performance, and ensure a seamless user experience. This section explores the complexities of scaling infrastructure and resources in mobile app development, including strategies for effective scaling, the challenges encountered, and the impact on app performance and user satisfaction.

Scaling infrastructure refers to adjusting and expanding an app's technical resources and architecture to accommodate growth in user numbers, data volume, and transaction intensity. This includes server capacity, database management, content delivery networks, and other backend components that ensure the app functions smoothly. Properly scaling infrastructure is critical to preventing downtime, slow performance, and other issues negatively affecting user retention and satisfaction.

One of the key strategies for scaling infrastructure is the implementation of cloud-based services. Cloud computing offers flexibility, scalability, and cost-effectiveness, allowing developers to adjust resources dynamically in response to changing demands. Services like Amazon Web Services (AWS), Google Cloud Platform (GCP), and Microsoft Azure provide a range of scalable computing resources, from server space to database services, that can be tailored to the specific needs of an app. Cloud services also facilitate global distribution, ensuring users across different regions experience consistent app performance.

Another critical aspect of scaling is optimizing database performance. As user numbers grow, so does the volume of data processed and stored. Efficient database management and scaling are necessary to ensure fast query responses and data integrity. This can involve techniques such as database sharding, where data is partitioned across multiple servers to distribute the load, and indexing, which speeds up data retrieval. Additionally, leveraging in-memory data stores for frequently accessed data can significantly enhance performance.

Load balancing is also a vital component of scaling infrastructure. It involves distributing incoming app traffic across multiple servers to prevent any single server from becoming overwhelmed, thereby maintaining app responsiveness and reliability. Load balancers can dynamically allocate resources based on real-time traffic patterns, ensuring optimal performance even during peak usage times.

Implementing a microservices architecture can further facilitate scaling by breaking down the app into a collection of smaller, independent services. This approach allows for individual components of the app to be scaled as needed without affecting the entire system. Microservices architecture enhances agility, making updating and improving specific app parts easier without significant downtime or disruptions.

Despite the clear benefits, scaling infrastructure and resources in mobile app development presents several challenges. One of the primary challenges is predicting growth and scaling needs accurately. Underestimating growth can lead to insufficient resources and poor app performance, while overestimating can result in unnecessary costs. Achieving a balance requires careful planning, monitoring, and the ability to quickly adapt to app usage and growth patterns.

Cost management is another significant challenge. Scaling infrastructure, particularly in a rapid growth phase, can be expensive. Developers must strategically plan their scaling efforts to optimize costs without compromising on performance. This includes selecting the right cloud services and pricing models, efficient resource utilization, and regularly auditing infrastructure costs to identify potential savings.

Security and compliance issues also become more complex as infrastructure scales. With an increase in data volume and user activity, ensuring data privacy, security, and compliance with regulations such as GDPR becomes increasingly challenging. Developers must implement robust security measures, including encryption, access controls, and regular security audits, to protect user data and maintain trust.

In conclusion, scaling infrastructure and resources is a critical aspect of mobile app development that directly impacts the app's performance, user experience, and overall success. Effective scaling strategies, including leveraging cloud-based services, optimizing database performance, implementing load balancing, and adopting a microservices architecture, are essential for managing growth efficiently. However, developers must navigate challenges such as predicting growth accurately, managing costs, and ensuring security and compliance. By resolving these challenges and adopting a proactive approach to scaling, developers can ensure their apps remain reliable, performant, and capable of supporting a growing user base.

Expanding to New Markets

Expanding to new markets is a critical strategy for mobile app businesses seeking to increase their user base, revenue, and brand presence. In a globalized digital economy, the potential to reach users across different regions and demographics has never been more accessible. However, this expansion comes with its own set of challenges, including cultural differences, regulatory requirements, and localization needs. This section delves into the strategic considerations, benefits, and challenges of expanding to new markets in the mobile app business, offering insights into how developers can navigate this complex landscape successfully.

Several factors, including market saturation in current regions, identification of untapped user segments, and opportunities for growth in emerging markets drive the decision to expand to new markets. Expansion opens new revenue streams and diversifies the app's user base, reducing dependency on a single market and mitigating risks associated with market-specific downturns. Furthermore, entering new markets can enhance the app's brand recognition and competitiveness on a global scale.

A successful market expansion strategy begins with thorough market research to identify promising regions for the app. This involves analyzing market size, user behavior, competition, and growth potential. Understanding local preferences, cultural nuances, and language requirements is crucial to assess the app's fit and adaptability to the new market. Additionally, developers must consider the regulatory landscape of the target market, including data protection laws, app store regulations, and any other legal requirements that might impact the app's launch and operation.

Localization is a key component of preparing an app for a new market. Beyond translating the app's content into the local language, localization encompasses adapting the app's features, design, and user experience to meet users' cultural and functional expectations in the new market. This might include modifying content, adjusting currency and payment methods, and redesigning user interfaces to align with local preferences. Effective localization ensures the app resonates with the target audience, increasing the likelihood of adoption and engagement.

Marketing and user acquisition strategies must also be tailored to the new market. This involves leveraging local media channels, social media platforms, and influencer networks to generate awareness and interest in the app. Collaborating with local partners, such as other app developers, businesses, or community organizations, can provide valuable insights and support in reaching the target audience. Customizing marketing messages and campaigns to reflect local values, trends, and language can significantly enhance their effectiveness.

Another consideration for expanding to new markets is the app's infrastructure and support capabilities. Ensuring the app can handle increased and potentially varied traffic from different regions is essential for maintaining performance and user satisfaction. This might involve scaling server capacity, optimizing load balancing, and implementing content delivery networks (CDNs) to improve app speed and reliability. Additionally, providing user support in the local language and adjusting support hours to accommodate different time zones are essential for delivering a positive user experience.

Despite the potential benefits, expanding to new markets presents challenges. Cultural missteps can occur if the app's content or marketing efforts fail to consider local sensibilities, leading to negative user reactions.

Navigating the regulatory requirements of new markets can also be complex and time-consuming. Furthermore, competition in the new market may be fierce, requiring significant effort and resources to establish a foothold.

To mitigate these challenges, developers should prioritize markets with the highest possibility for success based on their research. Engaging local experts, such as legal advisors, marketing professionals, and cultural consultants, can provide valuable guidance and insights. Developers should also adopt a phased approach to expansion, starting with a pilot launch in the new market to gather feedback and make necessary adjustments before a full-scale rollout.

In conclusion, expanding to new markets is a strategic move that can drive growth as well as diversification for mobile app businesses. Developers can increase their chances of successful expansion by carefully selecting target markets, localizing the app to meet the needs and expectations of new users, and tailoring marketing strategies to the local context. While challenges such as cultural differences, regulatory hurdles, and competition are inevitable, thorough preparation, local partnerships, and a flexible approach to market entry can help navigate these obstacles. Ultimately, expanding to new markets offers the opportunity to reach new users, enhance brand presence, and achieve sustained growth in the global app ecosystem.

Strategic Partnerships and Acquisitions

Strategic partnerships and acquisitions represent pivotal moves in the lifecycle of a mobile app business, offering pathways to growth, market expansion, and enhanced technological capabilities. These strategic decisions can significantly influence an app's success trajectory, facilitating access to new user bases, resources, and expertise. This section delves into the nuances of forming strategic partnerships and navigating acquisitions in the mobile app business, examining their benefits, the considerations involved in making such decisions, and strategies for maximizing their potential.

Strategic partnerships in the mobile app industry are collaborations between businesses that aim to leverage each other's strengths to achieve common goals. These partnerships can vary widely in form and function, ranging from marketing collaborations, content-sharing agreements, and technology integrations to co-development projects. The significance of a successful partnership lies in the synergy between the partners' offerings, where the collaboration creates value greater than the sum of its parts. For mobile app businesses, partnerships can provide several advantages, including access to new markets, enhanced product offerings, increased brand visibility, and shared technological resources.

One of the major benefits of strategic partnerships is the ability to tap into new user bases. Mobile apps can significantly broaden their reach by partnering with businesses with complementary user demographics. For instance, a fitness tracking app partnering with a popular health food brand can gain exposure to health-conscious consumers, potentially converting them into new users. Similarly, technology integrations with established platforms can enhance an app's functionality and appeal, such as integrating a payment app with a popular e-commerce platform to streamline user transactions.

Acquisitions, on the other hand, involve purchasing one business by another. For mobile app businesses, acquisitions can be a strategic move to accelerate growth, acquire new technologies, eliminate competition, or enter new markets rapidly. Acquisitions can also provide access to the acquired company's talent, intellectual property, and infrastructure, which can be invaluable assets in scaling operations and enhancing the app's offerings.

However, acquisitions present unique challenges and considerations. Identifying a suitable acquisition target involves thorough due diligence and evaluating the target company's financial health, user base, technology stack, and cultural fit. Negotiating the terms of the acquisition, such as the purchase price, integration plans, and roles of the key personnel post-acquisition, requires careful planning and negotiation. Furthermore, the post-acquisition integration process is critical to realizing the anticipated benefits of the acquisition, involving the alignment of technologies, processes, and corporate cultures.

Mobile app businesses should adhere to several key strategies to maximize the benefits of strategic partnerships and acquisitions. First, clearly defining the objectives and criteria for partnerships or acquisitions is essential. This clarity helps in identifying potential partners or acquisition targets that align with the business's strategic goals. For partnerships, establishing mutually beneficial terms and maintaining open communication channels are crucial for fostering a successful collaboration. Regular reviews of the partnership's outcomes against the set objectives can ensure that both parties remain aligned and responsive to changing market dynamics.

Conducting thorough due diligence cannot be overstated in the context of acquisitions. Understanding the intricacies of the target company's operations, financials, user engagement metrics, and potential synergies can prevent costly mistakes. Post-acquisition, a well-planned integration strategy that respects the strengths of the acquired company while aligning it with the broader strategic goals of the acquiring business is key to a successful merger.

Despite the potential benefits, strategic partnerships and acquisitions are not without risks. Partnerships can falter if objectives diverge or if the collaboration fails to deliver the expected value. Acquisitions can lead to integration challenges, cultural clashes, and distraction from the core business. Therefore, a cautious, strategic approach, coupled with rigorous planning and execution, is paramount.

In conclusion, strategic partnerships and acquisitions offer mobile app businesses valuable pathways to growth, innovation, and competitive advantage. Whether through leveraging complementary strengths in a partnership or accelerating growth through an acquisition, these strategic moves can significantly impact an app's market position and success. However, the key to leveraging these strategies effectively lies in careful planning, alignment with strategic objectives, and meticulous execution. By navigating these complex processes thoughtfully, mobile app businesses can unlock new opportunities, enhance their offerings, and achieve sustained growth in the dynamic app marketplace.

Managing Growth and Sustainability

Managing growth and sustainability in a mobile app business presents a unique set of challenges and opportunities. As the app gains traction, developers and business owners must navigate the complexities of scaling operations, maintaining quality, and ensuring long-term viability. This section explores the strategies for managing growth and ensuring sustainability in the competitive landscape of mobile app development, covering aspects such as user engagement, monetization, infrastructure scaling, and continuous innovation.

The initial success of a mobile app, marked by increasing downloads and active users, signals the onset of growth. However, managing this growth effectively requires a strategic approach to ensure that the app continues to meet user expectations while remaining financially viable. One of the first considerations in this phase is enhancing and maintaining user engagement. Developers must implement features and content that encourage regular use and deepen user investment in the app as the user base grows. Personalization, gamification, and regular updates with new content or functionalities can significantly improve engagement and retention rates.

Monetization strategy plays a crucial role in the sustainability of a mobile app business. While initial growth might be driven by user acquisition, long-term sustainability depends on generating consistent revenue. Diversifying revenue streams through a combination of advertising, in-app purchases, subscriptions, and partnerships can provide financial stability. Each monetization method comes with its advantages and challenges, and the choice of strategy should align with the app's value proposition and user preferences. For instance, subscription models may work well for content-driven apps, while in-app purchases might be more suitable for gaming apps.

As the app grows, scaling the infrastructure to handle increased traffic and data becomes essential. This includes expanding server capacity, optimizing databases, and ensuring that the app's architecture is scalable. Cloud-based services offer flexibility and scalability, allowing developers to adjust resources dynamically based on demand. Implementing robust data analytics and monitoring tools can also help anticipate scaling needs and identify potential bottlenecks before they impact user experience.

Maintaining high performance and reliability is paramount as the app scales. Users expect seamless functionality, fast load times, and minimal downtime. Implementing best practices in code optimization, caching strategies, and load balancing can help in achieving these performance goals. Additionally, establishing a rigorous testing process, including automated, stress, and beta testing with real users, can identify as well as resolve issues before they affect the broader user base.

Continuous innovation is another key factor in managing growth and ensuring sustainability. The mobile app market is highly dynamic, with evolving user expectations and technological advancements. To stay relevant and competitive, developers must continuously seek to improve the app and introduce new features that meet user needs. This requires staying attuned to market trends, gathering and analyzing user feedback, and being willing to pivot or adapt the app's direction in response to feedback and changing market conditions.

User feedback and data-driven decision-making should underpin the app's development and growth strategy. Collecting feedback through in-app surveys, user reviews, and social media can offer valuable insights into user needs, preferences, and pain points. Analyzing usage data can also reveal patterns and trends that inform feature development, marketing strategies, and monetization efforts. Engaging with the user community and fostering a sense of ownership among users can also drive loyalty and advocacy, further supporting growth and sustainability.

However, managing growth also involves addressing challenges such as increased competition, user churn, and resource constraints. As the app grows, attracting and retaining users becomes more challenging in a crowded market. Developing a strong brand, delivering exceptional value, and implementing effective marketing and user acquisition strategies are crucial for standing out. Additionally, managing resource allocation between user acquisition, development, and operations requires careful planning and prioritization to ensure sustainable growth and does not compromise the app's quality or financial health.

In conclusion, managing growth and ensuring sustainability in a mobile app business requires a multifaceted approach that balances user engagement, monetization, technical scalability, and continuous innovation. Developers can navigate growth challenges and build a sustainable, successful app business by focusing on delivering value to users, diversifying revenue streams, scaling infrastructure intelligently, and staying responsive to market trends and user feedback. As the app landscape evolves, flexibility, user-centricity, and strategic planning will remain key drivers of long-term success and sustainability.

CHAPTER X

Case Studies

Successful Mobile App Stories

The landscape of mobile app development is dotted with remarkable success stories that have not only transformed industries but also changed the way we live, work, and connect. These stories offer valuable insights into creativity, market understanding, and strategic execution. This section explores several successful mobile app stories, highlighting the innovative ideas, challenges overcome, and strategic decisions that led to their remarkable success.

One of the most iconic success stories is that of Instagram. Launched in 2010 by Kevin Systrom and Mike Krieger, Instagram started as a simple photo-sharing app with distinctive filters and social networking features. Its intuitive design, focus on visual content, and seamless social integration quickly captured users' interest, making it a fast-growing platform. Instagram's success caught the attention of Facebook, which acquired it for $1 billion in 2012. Today, Instagram is not merely a social media platform but a powerful tool for digital marketing, storytelling, and community building, illustrating the potential of a simple, user-focused app to revolutionize how people share and consume content.

Another exemplary success story is Spotify. Launched in 2008 by Daniel Ek and Martin Lorentzon, Spotify transformed the music industry by offering a legal streaming service that provided users with unlimited access to a enormous library of music for a subscription fee. Spotify's success lies in its innovative business model, which balanced the interests of artists, record labels, and listeners, and its personalized user experience, including curated playlists and recommendations. By addressing piracy concerns and changing how people accessed music, Spotify achieved tremendous growth and played a pivotal role in reshaping the music industry's revenue models.

WhatsApp's story is a testament to the power of simplicity and user privacy. Founded in 2009 by Brian Acton and also Jan Koum, WhatsApp offered a straightforward, reliable, and secure messaging experience, free from ads and gimmicks. Its focus on privacy, end-to-end encryption, and cross-platform functionality resonated with users worldwide, leading to rapid organic growth. Facebook's acquisition of WhatsApp for $19 billion in 2014 marked one of the largest deals in tech history, underlining the app's massive impact and the value of user trust and simplicity in design.

Uber's launch in 2009 revolutionized urban mobility by connecting passengers with drivers through a simple app, making transportation as easy as tapping a button. Founded by Garrett Camp and Travis Kalanick, Uber's innovative use of technology to offer real-time ride-hailing services, dynamic pricing, and a seamless payment experience addressed significant gaps in traditional taxi services. Despite facing regulatory hurdles and competition, Uber's focus on user convenience, safety features, and expansion into food delivery and freight services have solidified its position as a leader in the sharing economy.

The success of Pokémon GO, developed by Niantic, Inc., showcases the potential of augmented reality (AR) and gamification. Launched in 2016, Pokémon GO became an instant phenomenon, encouraging users to explore their surroundings to catch virtual Pokémon characters. The app's innovative use of AR, its social features, and the nostalgic appeal of the Pokémon brand contributed to its viral success, demonstrating how emerging technologies could create immersive and engaging user experiences.

These success stories share common innovation, user-centric design, and strategic adaptation themes. Instagram capitalized on the rising trend of mobile photography and social sharing, Spotify addressed the challenges of music piracy with a compelling legal alternative, WhatsApp prioritized user privacy and simplicity, Uber leveraged technology to disrupt traditional transportation, and Pokémon GO explored the possibilities of AR in gaming. Each story underscores the importance of understanding user needs, leveraging technology creatively, and being willing to adapt and evolve in response to market feedback and trends.

In conclusion, the successful mobile app stories of Instagram, Spotify, WhatsApp, Uber, and Pokémon GO offer valuable lessons for aspiring app developers and entrepreneurs. They illustrate that success in the mobile app industry requires more than just a good idea; it requires a profound understanding of the market, a commitment to user experience, and the agility to adapt and innovate continuously. By drawing inspiration from these stories, future app developers can navigate the challenges of the competitive app landscape and potentially create the next groundbreaking mobile app.

Lessons Learned from Failures

Failures in mobile app development offer valuable insights and lessons that can inform future endeavors, helping developers and businesses avoid common pitfalls and improve their chances of success. This section delves into the lessons learned from failures in mobile app development, highlighting the key reasons for failure, the implications for app developers, and strategies for mitigating risks.

One of the primary reasons for failure in mobile app development is a lack of market understanding. Many failed apps suffer from a disconnect between the app's features and user needs or preferences. Developers may build apps based on assumptions or personal preferences without conducting thorough market research or user validation. Consequently, the app may fail to gain traction or struggle to retain users, leading to eventual abandonment. The lesson here is the importance of understanding the target audience, identifying pain points, and validating app concepts through user feedback and market research before investing significant resources into development.

Another common reason for failure is poor user experience (UX) and design. In today's competitive app market, users have high expectations for usability, aesthetics, and performance. Apps with confusing navigation, cluttered interfaces, or slow loading times are likely to frustrate users and drive them to alternative options. Moreover, apps that fail to provide value or solve a specific problem for users are unlikely to succeed. The lesson learned is the crucial importance of investing in UX/UI design, prioritizing simplicity, intuitiveness, and functionality to make a positive user experience that keeps users engaged and satisfied.

Technical challenges and performance issues are also frequent culprits behind app failures. Apps that crash frequently, suffer from slow loading times, or drain battery life quickly are unlikely to retain users. Poorly optimized code, inefficient resource management, and inadequate testing practices can lead to these technical shortcomings. The lesson here is the necessity of prioritizing performance, scalability, and reliability throughout the development process. This includes rigorous testing across different devices and operating systems, optimizing code for efficiency, and leveraging scalable infrastructure to handle increased traffic and data volume.

Monetization strategy is another area where many apps stumble. Failing to establish a viable revenue model or implementing monetization tactics that alienate users can lead to financial struggles and eventual failure. For instance, apps that rely solely on advertising revenue may annoy users with intrusive ads, leading to uninstallation. Likewise, apps that charge too much for premium features or subscriptions may struggle to attract paying customers. The lesson learned is the importance of balancing user value with revenue generation, exploring multiple monetization avenues, and adapting the strategy based on user feedback and market dynamics.

Lastly, inadequate marketing and user acquisition efforts often contribute to app failures. Even the best-designed and most useful apps are unlikely to succeed without effective promotion and visibility. Many app developers underestimate the significance of marketing or rely solely on organic discovery, leading to low user acquisition and limited growth. The lesson here is that successful apps require strategic marketing efforts, including app store optimization, social media marketing, influencer partnerships, and targeted advertising campaigns. Building a strong brand, creating compelling app store listings, and actively engaging with users can significantly increase app visibility and downloads.

In conclusion, failures in mobile app development offer valuable lessons that can guide future endeavors and increase the likelihood of success. By understanding the common reasons for failure, such as a lack of market understanding, poor user experience, technical challenges, monetization issues, and inadequate marketing, developers can take proactive steps to mitigate risks and improve their app's chances of success. Embracing user-centric design principles, investing in robust development practices, adopting flexible monetization strategies, and implementing effective marketing tactics are essential for building sustainable and successful mobile apps in today's competitive landscape.

Analyzing Industry Trends

Analyzing industry trends in mobile app development is crucial for remaining ahead in the dynamic and competitive landscape of the app market. Mobile technology continues to evolve rapidly, driven by hardware, software, and user behavior advancements. This section explores some of the key industry trends shaping mobile app development, including the rise of 5G technology, the growing popularity of artificial intelligence (AI) and machine learning (ML), the emergence of immersive technologies including augmented reality (or AR) and virtual reality (or VR), and the increasing focus on privacy and security.

One of the most important trends in mobile app development is the rollout of 5G technology. As 5G networks become more widespread, developers have an opportunity to create apps with faster speeds, lower latency, and higher bandwidth. This opens up possibilities for richer multimedia experiences, real-time gaming, seamless video streaming, and new applications in areas like augmented reality (AR) and Internet of Things (IoT). Developers must adapt to this trend by optimizing their apps for 5G networks and exploring new use cases that leverage the capabilities of this technology to deliver enhanced user experiences.

Artificial intelligence (AI) and machine learning (ML) also reshape mobile app development. AI-powered features such as voice assistants, personalized recommendations, as well as predictive analytics are becoming increasingly common in mobile apps, offering users more intuitive and customized experiences. ML algorithms enable apps to analyze huge amounts of data, detect patterns, and make a data-driven decisions in real-time. Developers are integrating AI and ML capabilities into various apps, from productivity tools to healthcare apps, to enhance functionality, improve efficiency, and deliver more value to users.

Another trend gaining momentum is adopting immersive technologies like augmented reality (or AR) and virtual reality (or VR). AR and VR apps are transforming gaming, entertainment, education, and retail industries by creating immersive and interactive experiences. AR apps overlay digital data onto the physical realm, while VR apps transport users to virtual environments, enabling them to explore and interact with digital content in new ways. As hardware devices become more affordable and accessible, developers are exploring innovative applications of AR and VR in areas such as training simulations, virtual tourism, product visualization, and immersive storytelling.

Privacy and security have also become top priorities in mobile app development, driven by increasing concerns about data privacy and cyber threats. With regulations including California Consumer Privacy Act (CCPA) and General Data Protection Regulation (GDPR) imposing strict data handling and user consent requirements, developers must prioritize user privacy as well as implement strong security measures in their apps. This includes adopting encryption protocols, implementing secure authentication methods, and providing users with transparent privacy controls and data management options. Failure to address privacy and security concerns can result in reputational damage, legal liabilities, and loss of user trust.

In conclusion, analyzing industry trends in mobile app development is essential for staying competitive and meeting the evolving needs of users and businesses. From the rollout of 5G technology to integrating AI and ML capabilities, the emergence of immersive technologies like AR and VR, and the increasing focus on privacy and security, developers must stay updated about the latest trends and technologies shaping the industry. By embracing these trends and adjusting their strategies accordingly, developers can create innovative, user- centric apps that deliver value, drive engagement, and remain relevant in an ever-changing mobile landscape.

CHAPTER XI

Looking Ahead

Emerging Technologies and Trends

Emerging technologies as well as trends in mobile app development are constantly reshaping the landscape, offering developers new opportunities to innovate and deliver enhanced user experiences. This section explores some of the most impactful emerging technologies as well as trends that are shaping the future of mobile app development, including the Internet of Things (IoT), wearables, edge computing, blockchain, and progressive web apps (PWAs).

The Internet of Things (IoT) is revolutionizing how we interact with devices and data, and mobile apps are necessary in enabling this connectivity. IoT devices, ranging from smart home appliances and wearable fitness trackers to industrial sensors and connected vehicles, generate vast amounts of data that can be accessed and controlled through mobile apps. Developers are leveraging IoT technology to create apps that offer seamless integration with connected devices, enabling users to monitor and manage their environments remotely. This trend opens up new opportunities for innovative applications in areas such as home automation, healthcare, transportation, and smart cities.

Wearables represent another significant trend in mobile app development, driven by the proliferation of wearable devices including smartwatches, fitness trackers, as well as augmented reality glasses. Wearable apps give users real-time access to personalized health data, notifications, and contextual information, enhancing convenience and productivity. Developers are exploring novel use cases for wearables, such as fitness coaching, medical monitoring, navigation assistance, and augmented reality gaming. Integrating wearable technology with mobile apps offers opportunities to create more immersive, context-aware experiences that seamlessly blend the physical and digital worlds.

Edge computing is appearing as a transformative technology in mobile app development, enabling apps to process and evaluate data closer to the source, minimizing latency and improving performance. Edge computing leverages decentralized computing resources located at the network's edge, such as IoT devices, routers, and edge servers, to perform data processing tasks locally instead of relying solely on centralized cloud servers. This trend is particularly relevant for mobile apps that require real-time responsiveness, low latency, and offline functionality. By offloading computational tasks to edge devices, developers can create faster, more efficient apps that deliver superior user experiences, even in environments with limited connectivity.

Blockchain technology is gaining traction in mobile app development, offering decentralized and secure solutions for data management, identity verification, and transaction processing. Mobile apps powered by blockchain technology enable secure peer-to-peer transactions, transparent supply chain tracking, decentralized finance (DeFi) applications, and digital asset management. Developers are integrating blockchain features into mobile apps to enhance security, transparency, and trust, enabling users to confirm the integrity of data and transactions without relying on intermediaries. As blockchain technology matures and becomes even more accessible, its potential applications in mobile app development are expected to expand further.

Progressive web apps (PWAs) are emerging as a compelling alternative to native mobile apps, offering the benefits of web-based development while providing a native app-like experience to users. PWAs leverage modern web technologies including service workers, web app manifests, and responsive design to deliver fast, reliable, and engaging experiences across devices and platforms. Unlike traditional web apps, PWAs can be installed on users' devices, accessed offline, and integrated with device features like push notifications and geolocation. This trend empowers developers to create lightweight, cross-platform apps that offer the reach of the web and the functionality of native apps, without the need for app store distribution or installation barriers.

In conclusion, emerging technologies and trends in mobile app development are reshaping the future of digital experiences, offering developers unprecedented opportunities to create innovative, immersive, and intelligent apps. From the Internet of Things (IoT) and wearables to edge computing, blockchain, and progressive web apps (PWAs), these technologies are driving the evolution of mobile app development, enabling developers to deliver more personalized, efficient, and secure experiences to users. By embracing these trends and staying knowledgeable of the latest advancements, developers can unlock new possibilities and stay competitive in an ever-changing landscape.

Future of Mobile Apps

The future of mobile apps is poised to be transformative, characterized by technological advancements, shifts in user behavior, and the evolution of the digital ecosystem. This section explores several key trends and developments shaping the future of mobile apps, including the rise of artificial intelligence (or AI) and machine learning (or ML), the proliferation of augmented reality (or AR) and virtual reality (or VR), the emergence of 5G technology, the increasing focus on privacy and security, and the evolution of app development tools and platforms.

Artificial intelligence (AI) and machine learning (ML) are expected to play a central role in the future of mobile apps, enabling more intelligent, personalized, and context-aware experiences. Predictive analytics, natural language processing (or NLP), as well as computer vision are examples of AI-powered features that can improve app performance, automate processes, and provide consumers more relevant recommendations. Apps may now dynamically adjust to the tastes and actions of users due to machine learning algorithms' ability to scan enormous volumes of data and find patterns and insights. We anticipate a broad adoption of intelligent features in mobile apps across a range of industries, from healthcare as well as banking to retail and entertainment, as AI and ML technologies develop and become more widely available.

With their ability to combine the real and virtual worlds, AR and VR have the potential to completely change the way we use smartphone apps. AR apps overlay digital information onto the real-world environment, while VR apps transport users to virtual environments, enabling them to explore and interact with digital content in new ways. These technologies have applications in gaming, marketing, education, training, and beyond, offering opportunities for innovative storytelling, product visualization, and user engagement. As AR and VR hardware becomes more affordable as well as accessible, we can expect to see a surge in the adoption of immersive experiences in mobile apps, driving new forms of entertainment, communication, and commerce.

The rollout of 5G technology is expected to accelerate the adoption of mobile apps by enabling faster speeds, lower latency, and higher bandwidth. 5G networks will unlock new possibilities for mobile app developers, enabling more bandwidth-intensive applications, real-time streaming, and seamless device connectivity. With 5G, we can expect to see the proliferation of high-definition video streaming, cloud gaming, augmented reality experiences, and IoT applications that require ultra-low latency and reliable connectivity. As 5G networks become more widespread, developers must optimize their apps to take advantage of the increased speed and capacity, delivering users richer, more immersive experiences.

Future mobile app development will continue to place a high premium on privacy and security due to growing worries about data privacy, cyberthreats, and legal obligations. To prevent unwanted access and security breaches, developers must utilize strong security methods including data anonymization, authentication, and encryption. Differential privacy and federated learning are two examples of privacy-enhancing technologies that will play a bigger role in protecting user privacy while maintaining personalized experiences. Developers must place a high priority on transparency, user control, and compliance with privacy rules as laws like the CCPA (California Consumer Privacy Act) and the GDPR, or General Data Protection Regulation, impose tougher restrictions on data management and user consent.

Technological developments in app development platforms and tools will also influence the future of mobile app development by simplifying the process for developers to create and distribute apps for various platforms and devices. Low-code and no-code development platforms empower citizen developers and small businesses to create apps without extensive coding knowledge. Cross-platform development frameworks, including React Native and Flutter, enable developers to build apps that run seamlessly on iOS and Android devices, lessening development time and costs. Cloud-based development tools and services are facilitating collaboration, scalability, and continuous integration and delivery (CI/CD), enabling faster and more efficient app development cycles.

In conclusion, the future of mobile apps holds immense potential for innovation, disruption, and growth. With advancements in AI and ML, the proliferation of AR and VR, the rollout of 5G technology, the increasing focus on privacy and security, and the evolution of app development tools and platforms, we can expect to see a new era of mobile experiences that are more intelligent, immersive, and secure than ever before. By embracing these trends and leveraging the current technologies, developers can create apps that meet users' evolving needs and expectations in an increasingly digital realm.

Recommendations for Aspiring App Entrepreneurs

For aspiring app entrepreneurs, embarking on the journey of establishing and launching a successful mobile app can be both exhilarating and daunting. In order to help potential app entrepreneurs overcome obstacles and increase their chances of success within the competitive app market, this section provides advice and insights.

First and foremost, aspiring app entrepreneurs should start by identifying a clear problem or need in the market that their app can address. Conducting a thorough market research and understanding the target audience's pain points, preferences, and behaviors is essential for developing a compelling app concept. By focusing on solving a specific problem or fulfilling a genuine need, entrepreneurs can ensure that their app provides value and resonates with users, increasing its possibilities of success in the market.

Once the app concept is defined, aspiring entrepreneurs should prioritize user-centric design and usability. Creating a seamless as well as intuitive user experience is critical for engaging users and retaining their interest over time. Investing in user interface (UI) and user experience (UX) design, conducting usability testing, and gathering feedback from early users can help entrepreneurs identify areas for improvement and refine their app's design to optimize usability and satisfaction.

In addition to focusing on the app's functionality and design, aspiring entrepreneurs should pay careful attention to their app's monetization strategy. There are various monetization models to consider, including freemium, subscription, in-app purchases, advertising, and sponsorship. Each model has its advantages and disadvantages, and the choice should be guided by the app's target audience, value proposition, and market dynamics. By selecting the right monetization strategy and implementing it effectively, entrepreneurs can generate revenue and ensure the financial sustainability of their app business.

Another crucial aspect for aspiring app entrepreneurs to consider is marketing and user acquisition. Building a great app is only half the battle; effectively promoting it and acquiring users is equally essential for success. Developing a comprehensive marketing strategy that entails app store optimization (ASO), social media marketing, influencer partnerships, content marketing, and targeted advertising can help entrepreneurs increase visibility, attract users, and drive app downloads. Moreover, fostering a strong brand identity and cultivating a loyal user community can help sustain long-term growth and engagement.

Furthermore, aspiring app entrepreneurs should embrace a mindset of continuous learning and iteration. The app market is dynamic and ever-evolving, requiring entrepreneurs to stay knowledgeable about the latest trends, technologies, and best practices. By staying curious, seeking feedback from users and industry experts, and iterating on their app based on insights and data, entrepreneurs can adapt to changing market conditions, address user needs, and stay competitive in the fast-paced app landscape.

Lastly, aspiring app entrepreneurs should be prepared for setbacks and challenges along the way. Building a successful app business takes time, perseverance, and resilience. It's necessary to approach the journey with patience, persistence, as well as a willingness to learn from failures and mistakes. Entrepreneurs can prevail over obstacles and achieve their goals by maintaining a positive attitude, staying focused on the long-term vision, and continually iterating and improving their app.

In conclusion, aspiring app entrepreneurs have a world of opportunity at their fingertips, but success requires careful planning, execution, and adaptability. By identifying a compelling app concept, prioritizing user-centric design and usability, selecting the right monetization strategy, implementing effective marketing and user acquisition tactics, embracing continuous learning and iteration, and maintaining resilience in the face of challenges, entrepreneurs can maximize their chances of building a successful and sustainable app business. With dedication, creativity, and perseverance, aspiring entrepreneurs can turn their app ideas into reality and create a meaningful influence in the mobile app market.

CONCLUSION

As we end "The Mobile App Mastery: Innovate, Design, and Thrive in the App Ecosystem," it's essential to reflect on the journey we've taken together and the knowledge we've acquired along the way. From the inception of an idea to the successful launch and growth of a mobile app business, this book has provided you with a comprehensive framework for navigating the dynamic world of mobile apps.

Throughout these pages, we've explored the evolution of mobile apps, dissected the app ecosystem, and delved into the creative process of ideation and innovation. We've discussed design principles, development fundamentals, monetization strategies, marketing tactics, user engagement techniques, and scaling strategies, equipping you with a robust toolkit for success.

Real-world case studies, successful app stories, and industry insights have enriched our exploration, offering valuable lessons and practical advice you can utilize to your app endeavors. Whether you're a seasoned developer seeking to enhance your skills or a novice entrepreneur embarking on your first app venture, this book has provided you with the knowledge, tools, and strategies necessary to thrive in the competitive app market.

As you embark on your journey in the app ecosystem, remember that innovation and adaptability are key. Stay curious, embrace change, and also never stop learning. Keep your users at the center of everything you do, and prioritize delivering exceptional experiences. Cultivate a growth mindset, and also be willing to iterate, experiment, and refine your approach.

Above all, remember that success in the app ecosystem is not just about building great apps but also about building great businesses. Stay concentrated on your goals, be resilient in the face of challenges, and surround yourself with a supportive network of peers, mentors, and collaborators.

With dedication, perseverance, and the knowledge you've gained from this book, you have everything you need to embark on a successful journey in the vibrant and ever-evolving world of mobile apps. Thank you for joining us on this adventure, and may your future endeavors be filled with innovation, creativity, and boundless success.

Thank you for buying and reading/ listening to our book. If you found this book useful/ helpful please take a few minutes and leave a review on the platform where you purchased our book. Your feedback matters greatly to us.